Man Makes Himself

by

V. Gordon Childe

A MENTOR BOOK
NEW AMERICAN LIBRARY
TIMES MIRROR
NEW YORK AND SCARBOROUGH, ONTARIO

Preface

THIS book is not intended to be a manual of archaeology, still less of the history of science. It is meant to be readable to those who are not concerned with the detailed problems about which specialists argue heatedly. It must therefore ignore such problems, and avoid, moreover, the technical terms and outlandish names that make textbooks on prehistory (including my own) scientific, but hard to follow. But to simplify the argument and the vocabulary I have had to sacrifice accuracy. Almost every statement in prehistory should be qualified by the phrase: "On the evidence available today the balance of probability favors the view that." The reader is hereby requested to insert this or some similar reservation in most of my statements. Not all my assertions would be generally accepted even with that qualification; but it has been impossible to cumber the text with detailed arguments irrelevant to the main thesis. I still contend that the facts are stated accurately enough for the purposes of this book, and that acceptable amendments would not affect the argument in any way. And finally I confess that, while Chapters IV to VII are based on first-hand study of the original objects, and reports, Chapter VIII uses exclusively translations and commentaries by competent authorities cited in the notes.

Contents

Illustrations

AN EGYPTIAN SAILING SHIP OF THE OLD KINGDOM.

CHAPTER I

HUMAN AND NATURAL HISTORY

Last century "progress" was accepted as a fact. Trade was expanding, the productivity of industry was increasing, wealth was accumulating. Scientific discoveries promised a boundless advance in man's control over Nature, and consequently unlimited possibilities of further production. Growing prosperity and deepening knowledge inspired an atmosphere of unprecedented optimism throughout the Western world. Now that optimism has received a rude shock. World War I and subsequent crises, producing even in the midst of horrible poverty an apparent surplus of goods, have undermined its economic foundations. Doubts as to the reality of "progress" are widely entertained.

To settle their doubts men should turn to history. But historians themselves are not unaffected by the economic situation of their day. As Professor Bury has shown, the idea of progress was itself a novelty, entirely foreign to medieval or ancient writers on history. Today in history, as in natural science, a pessimistic or mystical attitude is conspicuous in the writers of many popular authors. Some are inclined, like the Ancient Greeks and Romans, to look back wistfully to a "golden age" of primeval simplicity. The German "historical school" of Roman Catholic missionaries and their archaeological and anthropological instructors have revived and reclothed in scientific terms the medieval doctrine of the "Fall of Man" through tasting of the tree of knowledge. A similar outlook is implicit in some writings of the English diffusionists. On the other hand, the Fascist philosophy, expounded most openly by Herr Hitler and his academic supporters, but sometimes masquerading as eugenics in Britain and America, identifies progress with a biological evolution no less mystically conceived.

One purpose of this book is to suggest that, viewed from an impersonal scientific standpoint, history may still justify a belief in progress in days of depression as well as in the heyday of last century's prosperity. But to achieve the necessary scientific attitude we must be prepared to modify our conceptions both of progress and of history. The essence of the scientific attitude is, indeed, the abandonment of personal prejudices and the subordination of private likes and dislikes. "The function of science is the classification of facts, the recognition of their sequence and relative significance." The scientific attitude is shown in the habit of forming judgments on the facts unbiased by personal feeling. "The scientific man," says Karl Pearson, "has to strive at self-elimination in his judgments." Incidentally the importance attached by scientists to number and measurement is not unconnected with the obligation to adopt an impersonal attitude. "The results of measurement," as Professor Levy remarks, "will be entirely independent of any religious, ethical, or social bias. Whether you like or dislike the words on this page, you will agree that the number is 322."

To approach history in this humble and objective spirit is not so easy. As scientists we cannot ask History: "Have we progressed? Does the multiplication of mechanical devices represented by airplanes, hydroelectric stations, poison gas, and submarines constitute progress?" A question so formulated can have no scientific meaning. There is no hope of any agreement upon its answer. That would depend entirely upon the caprice of the inquirer, his economic situation at the time, and even on the state of his health. Very few people will come to the same conclusion.

If you like rapid movement and the freedom from limitations on time and space provided by modern facilities for locomotion and illumination, you may answer in the affirmative. But not unless you are in an economic position to enjoy such facilities, not if your lungs have been filled with mustard gas, or your son has just been blown to pieces with a shell. If you have a romantic affection for the "unspoiled countryside" and no passion for roaming far abroad or turning night into day for study, you will query the reality of a progress thus attested, and look back regretfully upon the "more peaceful" days of a century or two ago. You will conveniently forget the drawbacks to the simple life—the vermin in the picturesque thatch, the disease-germs swarming in contaminated wells and open middens, the bandits and the press-gangs lurking in the woods and alleys. Dumped down in a village in Turkestan, you might revise your opinion. A pickpocket must regard from his professional standpoint electric light, the telephone, and automobiles (if used by the police) as signs of regression. He will sigh for the dark and narrow alleys of a previous century. Persons devoted to the grosser forms of cruelty will not accept the suppression of legal torture and the elimination of public executions as signs of progress, but of the reverse.

It is unscientific to ask, "Have we progressed?," if only because no two people need give the same answer; the personal equation can hardly be eliminated. But it may be legitimate to ask, "What is progress?," and the answer may even take on something of the numerical form that science so rightly prizes. But now progress becomes what has actually happened—the content of history. The business of the historian would be to bring out the essential and significant in the long and complex series of events with which he is confronted. But to distinguish and unpick the thread of progress, if such there be, running through history requires a view of history very different from that set out in the formal textbooks in my schooldays. In the first place, a long and wide view is essential. When short periods or confined regions alone are surveyed, the multiplicity of separate events is likely to obscure any underlying pattern.

Before 1914, at least, history meant to most people "British history." It began with the Anglo-Saxons, or even with the Norman Conquest, and so embraced a period of at most 1500 and often 800 years. Quite a number of people were acquainted with another volume of history labeled "ancient history." It dealt with the fortunes of the Greeks (or more precisely of two Greek cities, Athens and Sparta) and of the Romans. It was generally presented and taught as if it had no vital connection with British history, from which it was separated by a mysterious gap. Many people are now aware that these two still popular volumes are not really self-contained and independent, but form a small part of a connected series. Such have at least heard of earlier volumes in which Minoans, Hittites, Egyptians, and Sumerians figure. The period covered by the whole series is now fully four times that of British history in the fullest sense. Quite recently prehistory has become familiar as an introductory volume. It traces the fortunes—or some aspects thereof—of peoples who kept no written records. In particular, it deals with the period before the earliest written documents begin in Egypt and Babylonia. By the inclusion of prehistory the purview of history is extended a hundredfold. We survey a period of over 500,000 years, instead of a beggarly 5000. And at the same time human history joins on to natural history. Through prehistory history is seen growing out of the "natural sciences" of biology, paleontology, and geology.

As long as history is restricted in its scope to comparatively brief periods like those of British history or ancient history, up and downs seem much more conspicuous than any steady progress. In ancient history we learnt about the "Rise and Fall" of Athens and Sparta and Rome. I confess I was not quite sure what was a "rise" and what a "fall." The history of Athens from 600 to 450 B.C. was presented as a rise, the next century as a fall. The subsequent centuries, omitted altogether from schoolbooks, were presumably an age of darkness and death. It was disconcerting to notice that Aristotle flourished near 325 B.C. and that some of the greatest Greek scientists—doctors, mathematicians, astronomers, and geographers—worked in the supposedly dead hinterland of "classical" Greek history. Greek civilization was not dead, though Athens had declined in political power; and Athens' contributions to a wider Hellenism survived. The "rise" of Rome was represented by the period during which, by ruthlessness and even fraud, a group of obscure villages on the Tiber became the capital of an empire embracing the whole Mediterranean basin, France, England, and a large slice of Central Europe. But eventfully this vast domain was pacified, and Rome secured to her subjects two centuries of comparative peace, unprecedented in Europe. But these centuries, discreetly omitted from schoolbooks, we were left to imagine as an era of "decline."

In British history the ups and downs are only slightly less glaring or more rational. The age of Elizabeth was "golden" because the English were successful as pirates against the Spaniards, burned chiefly Catholics at the stake, and patronized Shakespeare's plays. The seventeenth and eighteenth centuries were comparatively inglorious, though Newton adorned the former and James Watt the latter.

In fact, ancient history and British history tended to be presented exclusively as political history—a record of the maneuvers of kings, statesmen, soldiers, and religious teachers, of wars and persecutions, of the growth of political institutions and ecclesiastical systems. Incidental allusions were indeed made to economic conditions, scientific discoveries, or artistic movements in each "period," but the "periods" were defined in political terms by the names of dynasts or party factions. That sort of history could hardly become scientific. No standard of comparison is manifest in it independent of the prejudices of the individual teacher. The age of Elizabeth is "golden" primarily to a member of the Church of England. To a Roman Catholic period when Protestants were burned inevitably seem preferable. And such history restricts its own field hopelessly. Prehistory can find no place in it. For, since prehistory lacks all written evidence, it can never recover the names of its actors or discern the details of their private lives. It can seldom give names even to the peoples whose wanderings some prehistorians try to trace.

Fortunately the exclusive claim of political history to the

title is no longer unchallenged. Marx insisted on the prime importance of economic conditions, of the social forces of production, and of applications of science as factors in historical change. His realist conception of history is gaining acceptance in academic circles remote from the party passions inflamed by other aspects of Marxism. To the general public and to scholars alike, history is tending to become cultural history, greatly to the annoyance of fascists like Dr. Frick.

This sort of history can naturally be linked up with what is termed prehistory. The archaeologist collects, classifies, and compares the tools and weapons of our ancestors and forerunners, examines the houses they built, the fields they tilled, the food they ate (or rather discarded). These are the tools and instruments of production, characteristic of economic systems that no written document describes. Like any modern machine or construction, these ancient relics and monuments are applications of contemporary knowledge or science existing when they were fashioned. In a liner results of geology (oil, metal-ores), botany (timbers), chemistry (alloys, oil-refining), and physics (electrical equipment, engines, etc.) are combined, applied, and crystallized. That is equally true of the dugout canoe fashioned by Stone Age man from a single treetrunk.

Again, the ship and the tools employed in its production symbolize a whole economic and social system. The modern ship requires the assemblage at one centre of a variety of raw materials brought from many places, often distant; it presupposes an extensive and efficient system of communications. Its production involves the co-operation of large bodies of workers, each specialized in distinct crafts, but all acting together in accordance with a common plan and under centralized direction. Moreover, none of these workers are producing their own food by hunting, fishing, or farming. They are nourished by the surplus produced by other specialists devoted exclusively to the production or collection of foodstuffs, and again often living far away. The canoe, the lineal ancestor of our liner, also implies an economy, a social organization, but a very different and far simpler one. The only tool required is a stone adze that can be made at home by the worker out of a pebble from the nearest brook. The ship's timbers are provided by a local tree. In felling the tree, hewing it out, and dragging the result to the water, the co-operation of several workers may be necessary. But the numbers required are quite small, and need not exceed the bounds of a family group. Finally, a canoe may perfectly well be made by fishermen or peasants in the intervals of their primary avocation of getting food for

themselves and their children. It does not presuppose imported
foodstuffs, nor even an accumulated communal surplus, but
is a symbol of an economy of self-sufficing communities or
households. Such an economy can be seen at work today
among barbarous tribes. Archaeologists can define a period
when it was apparently the sole economy, the sole organization of production ruling anywhere on the earth's surface.
History, extended backwards by prehistory, can thus compare
the systems of production in vogue at widely separated points
in the great space of time it surveys.

Again, archaeology can observe changes in the economic
system, improvements in the means of production, and exhibit
them in a chronological sequence. The archaeologist's divisions of the prehistoric period into Stone, Bronze, and Iron
Ages are not altogether arbitrary. They are based upon the
materials used for cutting implements, especially axes, and
such implements are among the most important tools of production. Realistic history insists upon their significance in
molding and determining social systems and economic organization. Moreover, the stone axe, the tool distinctive of part
at least of the Stone Age, is the homemade product that could
be fashioned and used by anybody in a self-contained group
of hunters or peasants. It implies neither specialization of
labor nor trade beyond the group. The bronze axe which re-
places it is not only a superior implement, it also presupposes
a more complex economic and social structure. The casting of
bronze is too difficult a process to be carried out by anyone
in the intervals of growing or catching his food or minding
her babies. It is a specialist's job, and these specialists must
rely for such primary necessities as food upon a surplus produced by other specialists. Again, the copper and tin of which
the bronze axe is composed are comparatively rare, and very
seldom occur together. One or both of the constituents will
almost certainly have to be imported. Such importation is possible only if some sort of communications and trade have been
established and if there is a surplus of some local product to
barter for the metals (for details see p. 35).

To this extent the changes on which archaeologists are wont
to insist do correspond to the changes in forces of production,
in economic structure and social organization, which are
recorded in written documents and appreciated as fundamental by realist history. In fact, archaeology can and does trace
out radical changes in human economy, in the social system
of production. These changes are similar in kind to those upon
which the realist conception of history insists as factors in
historical change. In their effect upon humanity as a whole

some prehistoric changes at least are comparable to that dramatic transformation which is familiarly known as the Industrial Revolution of eighteenth-century Britain. Their significance must be estimated by the same criteria, their results judged by like standards. Indeed, an unbiased judgment may be easier in the case of prehistoric revolutions just because their effects have ceased to oppress us individually.

But not only does prehistory extend written history backwards, it carries on natural history forwards. In reality, if one root of prehistoric archaeology is ancient history, the other is geology. Prehistory constitutes a bridge between human history and the natural sciences of zoology, paleontology, and geology. Geology has traced the building up of the earth we inhabit; under the aspect of paleontology it follows the emergence of various forms of life through several vast periods of geological time. In the last era prehistory takes up the tale. Prehistoric anthropology, which is concerned with the bodily remains of early "men," is just a branch of paleontology or zoology. But prehistoric archaeology is concerned with what men made. It traces changes in human culture. Such changes, as will be shown in detail shortly, take the place of the physical modifications and mutations by which new species arise among the animals and which are studied in paleontology.

Hence the historian's "progress" may be the equivalent of the zoologist's evolution. It may be hoped that the standards applicable to the latter discipline may help the historian to attain the same impersonality and objectivity of judgment as characterize the zoologist or any other natural scientist. Now to a biologist progress, if he used the term, would mean success in the struggle for existence. Survival of the fittest is a good evolutionary principle. But fitness means just success in living. A provisional test of a species' fitness would be to count its members over several generations. If the total numbers turn out to be increasing, the species may be regarded as successful; if the total is dwindling, it is condemned as a failure.

Biologists have divided the organic world into kingdoms and sub-kingdoms. The latter are subdivided into phyla, phyla into classes and families, families into genera, genera into species. Paleontology traces the order in which the several phyla, genera, etc., emerge upon our planet. They are arranged in a sort of evolutionary hierarchy. In the animal kingdom the phylum chordata is ranked above the phyla protozoa (including germs, certain shellfish, and so on) and annulata (earthworms). Within the phylum, vertebrates occupy the highest place, and among the vertebrates mammals (warm-blooded animals that suckle their young) rank above fishes, birds, and reptiles. Rank here depends purely upon order of appearance. "Higher" means appearing later in the record of the rocks; in an ideal geological section the oldest forms of life would appear in the deepest layers, the last to emerge would be nearest the surface. Any departure from this purely chronological ranking is liable to involve the biologist in metaphysical controversies upon which, as a scientist, he is loath to embark. The historian might do well to follow his example.

Yet it may perhaps be permissible to suggest that values do in some cases attach to evoluntionary rank and that these values are capable of numerical expression. They may help to an appreciation of the significance of cultural change, if not to a vindication of progress in any metaphysical sense. The idea of fitness can scarcely be excluded altogether from biological rank, even though such fitness means just success in surviving. Of course, many lower forms still survive—all too successfully in the case of germs, very fortunately in the case of earthworms. On the other hand, the rocks reveal countless species, genera, and even families which have failed to survive, though in their day they would have ranked at the head of the evolutionary hierarchy. The gigantic reptiles like dinosaurs and ichthyosaurs, that swarmed during the Jurassic era, are now extinct. They flourished under particular geographical conditions. The Jurassic was an age of moist warm climate and wide expanses of sea and swamp; no more intelligent beasts existed to compete with the huge lizards. To these conditions, to this environment, the reptiles were successfully adapted. The same environment lasted for a time so long that estimates in years have no meaning. But eventually the areas under water became more restricted, the climate grew drier and colder, and new genera and species emerged. Comparatively few of the reptiles succeeded in surviving in the new environment. They could not adjust themselves to the changed conditions, and perished. When the old Jurassic environment passed, the very qualities which had ensured their success and constituted their "fitness" proved a handicap. They were too much specialized, too closely adapted for living under one limited set of conditions. With the passing of those conditions they succumbed. In the long run, too, excessive specialization is biologically disadvantageous. Its ultimate result is not survival, not increase in numbers, but extinction or stagnation.

Very tentatively, too, we might draw attention to the idea of economy in the means whereby survival is secured. Many of the lower organisms only survive, only maintain their numbers, by a prodigious fecundity. Each individual or pair produces millions of offspring. Yet the species is so poorly fitted to survive that only one or two out of every batch live to maturity. Cod, ling, and some other fish, for instance, have succeeded in keeping their numbers fairly constant over a vast period of time. To that extent they are successful. But to purchase this precarious balance a pair of cod produces 6,000,000 eggs, a pair of ling 28,000,000! If any substantial proportion of these eggs came to maturity, the sea would soon be a solid mass of ling. Actually only two or three ling hatch out and come to maturity from each batch. The individual egg's chance of survival or prospect of life is about 1 in 14,000,000. Rabbits are much more economical. A doe rabbit may produce seventy offspring annually. As the total rabbit population keeps fairly constant in the long run, the individual's chance of survival is clearly or the order of 1 in 70. A human pair does not produce more than one child a year, and families exceeding 10 are uncommon. Yet the human species is still increasing in numbers. The human child's chance of survival is incomparably greater than that of a young rabbit.

Within certain limits, economy in reproduction, the individual's chance of surviving increases as we ascend the evolutionary scale. And these concepts—fitness, chance of survival—are essentially numerical. In so far as they apply, they constitute criteria invested with all the objectivity of numbers for biological ranking. Unfortunately this argument must not be pressed. While some "lower organisms" secure survival by extravagant fecundity, others no less humble in the evolutionary scale exhibit as strict economy in reproduction as men or elephants, and yet maintain their numbers.

It would be unwise to pursue such discussions further, for fear of introducing ideas of value foreign to pure science. They have at least indicated that the continuity between natural history and human history may allow numerical concepts to be introduced into the latter. Historical changes can be judged by the extent to which they have helped our species to survive and multiply. That is a numerical criterion expressible in figures of population. In history we encounter events to which this numerical criterion is directly applicable. The most obvious instance is the "Industrial Revolution" in Britain. Estimates of the island's population indicate a quite gradual growth in the population from the Black Death in the fourteenth century. Reliable calculations put the population at 4,160,221 in 1570, 5,773,646 in 1670, and 6,517,035 in 1750. Then with the Industrial Revolution begins the dramatic increase to 16,345,646 in 1801 and 27,533,755 in 1851!

The effect of these figures is still more impressive if they be plotted out on squared paper to give a graph or "population curve." The general direction of the line is almost straight down to 1750, and unaffected by the political revolutions and religious movements of the sixteenth and seventeenth centuries that bulk so large in the old history books. Between 1750 and 1800 the line has turned through an angle of about 30°! The sweeping changes in material culture and equipment, the new

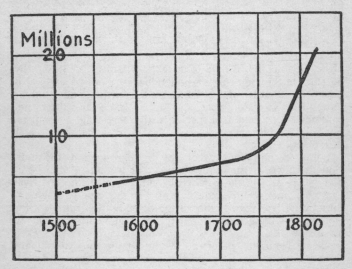

FIG. 1.—GRAPH OF THE ESTIMATED POPULATION OF
GREAT BRITAIN, 1500-1800.

social forces of production, the economic reorganization that is termed the Industrial Revolution, reacted upon the whole mass of the British people as no political or religious event had done. One effect obviously was to render possible a gigantic increase in their numbers. The people multiplied as never before since the arrival of the Saxons. Judged by the biological standard suggested above, the Industrial Revolution was a success. It has facilitated the survival and multiplication of the species concerned.

The figures provide an objective criterion by which such an event may be judged. It is useless to insist either on the lustre of the intellectual achievements in science which the new system of production alone made possible, or on the horrors of child-labor, slums, and oppression which accompanied it. The former may be cancelled by the latter. But the evils cannot be

seen in their true perspective for lack of standards of comparison. We happen to be well informed about the misery,
disease, and ugliness imposed upon the proletariat by the
factory system. We know surprisingly little of the real position
of the bulk of the peasantry, of miners, and of laborers in
previous centuries. While we know a good deal about the guilds
of urban artisans—really a relatively small and privileged
class—we dare not picture faithfully the life of a serf in the
Middle Ages, still less that of a slave in ancient Rome or
Greece. When a gleam of the truth shines from the page of a
medieval charter or an ancient oration, the sentimentalists
wisely close their eyes in utter horror. So on the whole we may
rely upon our figures.

And remembering the lesson of those figures and curves, we
shall be able to discern in earlier ages of human history other
"revolutions." They manifest themselves in the same way as
the "Industrial Revolution"—in an upward kink in the population curve. They must be judged by the same standard. The
chief aim of this book is to examine prehistory and ancient
history from this angle. It is hoped that a consideration of
revolutions, so remote that it is impossible to get angry or enthusiastic about them, may help to vindicate the idea of progress against sentimentalists and mystics.

CHAPTER II

ORGANIC EVOLUTION AND CULTURAL PROGRESS

IT HAS been suggested that prehistory is a continuation of natural history, that there is an analogy between organic evolution and progress in culture. Natural history traces the emergence of new species each better adapted for survival, more fitted to obtain food and shelter, and so to multiply. Human history reveals man creating new industries and new economies that have furthered the increase of his species and thereby vindicated its enhanced fitness.

The wild sheep is fitted for survival in a cold mountain climate by its heavy coat of hair and down. Men can adapt themselves to life in the same environment by making coats out of sheeps' skin or of wool. With claws and snouts rabbits can dig themselves burrows to provide shelter against cold and enemies. With picks and shovels men can excavate similar refuges, and even build better ones out of brick, stone, and timber. Lions have claws and teeth with which to secure the meat they need. Man makes arrows and spears for slaying his game. An innate instinct, an inherited adjustment of its rudimentary nervous system, enables even the lowly jellyfish to grasp prey that is actually within its reach. Men learn more efficient and discriminating methods of obtaining nourishment through the precept and example of their elders.

In human history, clothing, tools, weapons, and traditions take the place of fur, claws, tusks, and instincts in the quest for food and shelter. Customs and prohibitions, embodying centuries of accumulated experience and handed on by social tradition, take the place of inherited instincts in facilitating the survival of our species.

There certainly is an analogy. But it is essential not to lose sight of the significant distinctions between historical progress and organic evolution, between human culture and the animal's bodily equipment, between the social heritage and the biological inheritance. Figurative language, based on the admitted analogy, is liable to mislead the unwary. We read, for instance:

"In the Jurassic epoch the struggle for life must have been very severe. . . . *Triceratops* covered its head and neck with a kind of bony bonnet with two horns over the eyes." The passage suggests the sort of thing that happens conspicuously in wartime. Between 1915 and 1918, finding themselves threatened from the air, the belligerents devised shrapnel-helmets, anti-aircraft guns, bombproof shelters, and other protective contrivances. Now that process of invention is not in the least like the evolution of *Triceratops* as conceived by the biologists. Its bony bonnet was part of its body; it was inherited from its parents; it had been developed very slowly as a result of small spontaneous modifications in reptiles' body-covering that had been accumulating over hundreds of generations. It survived not because *Triceratops* liked it, but because those of his ancestors who possessed its rudiments had in actual practice succeeded better in acquiring food and eluding dangers than those that lacked this bodily equipment and protection. Man's equipment and defenses are external to his body; he can lay them aside and don them at will. Their use is not inherited, but learned, rather slowly, from the social group to which each individual belongs. Man's social heritage is a tradition which he begins to acquire only after he has emerged from his mother's womb. Changes in culture and tradition can be initiated, controlled, or delayed by the conscious and deliberate choice of their human authors and executors. An invention is not an accidental mutation of the germ plasm, but a new synthesis of the accumulated experience to which the inventor is heir by tradition only. It is well to be as clear as possible as to the sort of differences subsisting between the processes here compared.

The mechanism of evolution as conceived by biologists need not be described in detail. It has been outlined elsewhere in accessible and readable books by experts. The current view seems to be briefly something like this. The evolution of new forms of life and of new species among animals is supposed to result from the accumulation of hereditable changes in the germ plasm. (The exact nature of these changes is as obscure to scientists as are the words germ plasm to the ordinary reader.) Such changes as facilitated the life and reproduction of the creature would become established by what is termed "natural selection." The creatures not affected by the changes in questions would simply die out or become confined to some corner, leaving the new species in possession of the field. A concrete and partly fictitious example will illustrate the meaning better than several pages more of abstract terms.

About half a million years ago Europe and Asia were visited by periods of intense cold—the so-called Ice Ages—that lasted thousands of years. By that time there were in existence several species of elephant ancestral to modern African and Indian elephants. To meet the rigors of the Ice Age some elephants developed a shaggy coat of hair, becoming eventually what we term mammoths. This statement does not mean than an ordinary elephant said one day, "I feel horribly chilly; I will put on a shaggy coat," nor yet that by continually wishing for a coat it mysteriously made hairs to sprout out of its hide. What is supposed to have happened would be more like this:

The germ plasm is liable to change, and is constantly changing. Among the elephant calves born as the Ice Age was becoming severe were some that, as result of such a change in the germ plasm, were born with a tendency to hairy skins, and as they grew up actually became hairy. In the cold latitudes the hairy elephants would thrive better and rear larger families, also hairy, than the more normal type. They would accordingly increase at the expense of the rest. Moreover, similar mysterious changes in the germ plasm might result in some of their offspring being still more hairy than their ancestors and other contemporaries. These in their turn, being the best fitted to endure the cold, would thrive better and multiply faster than any others. And so, after many generations, a breed of hairy elephants or mammoths would be established as the result of the accumulation of the successive hereditary variations described. And such alone would be able to withstand the glacial conditions of northern Europe and Asia. The mammoth thus got his permanent shaggy coat, but as the result of a process extending over many generations and thousands of years—for elephants of all species are slow breeders.

During the Ice Ages several species of man already existed, contemporary with the mammoth: they hunted the beasts and drew pictures of them in caves. But they did not inherit shaggy coats and did not develop such to meet the crisis; some of the human inhabitants of Europe during the Ice Age would pass unrecognized in a crowd today. Instead of undergoing the slow physical changes which eventually enable the mammoths to endure the cold, our ancestors found out how to control fire and to make coats out of skins. And so they were able to face the cold as successfully as the mammoths.

Of course, while the mammoth-calf was born with a tendency to a hairy coat, which inevitably grew as the calf

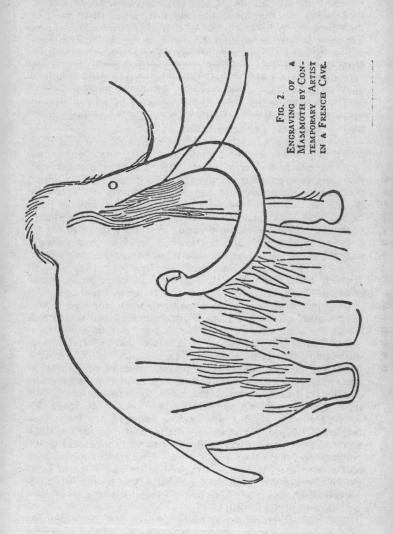

FIG. 2.
ENGRAVING OF A
MAMMOTH BY CON-
TEMPORARY ARTIST
IN A FRENCH CAVE.

matured, the human infant was not born as a fire tender or coat maker. The parent mammoths transmitted their coats to their progeny by heredity. Each generation of human children had to be taught the whole art of keeping fires going and making coats from the very rudiments. The art was transmitted from parent to child only by precept and example. It was an "acquired characteristic," and acquired characteristics, zoologists agree, are not hereditary. An infant by himself on his natal day is no more a fire tender than when, half a million years ago, man first began to cherish the flames instead of fleeing from them like other beasts.

The foregoing narrative could be translated into technical terms as follows: certain members of the genus *Elephas* became adapted to the environment of the Ice Ages, and evolved into the species *Elephas primigenius*. The species *Homo sapiens* was enabled to survive in the same environment by improving his material culture. Both evolution and cultural change may be regarded as adaptations to the environment. Environment, of course, means the whole situation in which a creature has to live: it embraces not only climate (heat, cold, moisture, wind) and physiographical features like mountains, seas, rivers, and marshes, but also factors such as food supplies, animal enemies, and, in the case of man, even social traditions, customs, and laws, economic status, and religious beliefs.

Both men and mammoths were successfully adjusted to the environment of the Ice Ages. Both flourished and multiplied under those peculiar climatic conditions. But their ultimate histories diverged. The last Ice Age passed, and with its passage the mammoth became extinct. Man has survived. The mammoth was too well adapted to a particular set of conditions; it was overspecialized. When, with the onset of more temperate conditions, forests covered the wide tundras on which the mammoth had roamed and temperate vegetation replaced the Arctic scrub on which the mammoth browsed, the beast was helpless. The bodily characters—hairy coat, digestive system adjusted to consume dwarf willows or mosses, hoofs and trunk constructed for rooting in the snow—which had enabled him to thrive in the Ice Ages, all proved to be handicaps in temperate climates. Man, on the other hand, was free to leave off his coat if he was too hot, to invent other tools, and to choose beef instead of mammoth steaks.

The last paragraph drives home a lesson already indicated. In the long run exclusive adaptation to a peculiar environment does not pay. It imposes severe, and in the end perhaps fatal, restrictions on the possibilities of living and breeding. On a long view what is profitable is the capacity for adaptation to changing circumstances. Such adaptability is bound up with the growth of a nervous system, and ultimately of a brain.

Even the lowest organism is equipped with a rudimentary nerve apparatus enabling it to make one or two simple movements in response to changes in the surrounding world. The external changes excite or stimulate what serves the creature as an "organ of sense," and this stimulation sets going certain determined movements or changes in the creature's body. The approach of a predatory bird—or of any other object—when impinging on the sense organ of an oyster stimulates its nerve in such a way as to cause a contraction of the muscles closing its shell. The oyster's nervous system provides it with a sort of automatic device for self-protection, but it has no power to vary the movement in accordance with differences in the external changes which promote it. The nervous system is adjusted to make one set of muscular movements whenever any external object affects its sensory ends. All automatic responses that an organism is adjusted to make to any changes in its environment may be termed instincts.[1] They are, of course, inherited in precisely the same way as the creature's physical form. They are necessary and inevitable consequences of the structure of its nervous system, which is part of its bodily mechanism.

The higher we go in the evolutionary scale, the more complicated the nervous system is found to be. Organs become specialized to detect different sorts of changes in the environment—pressures upon the creature's body, vibrations in the air, rays of light, and so on. Thus arise the distinct senses of touch, hearing, vision, and the rest, and appropriate bodily organs connected therewith. At the same time the number and variety of the movements that the creature can make are increased by the development and specialization of motor nerves controlling muscles or sets of muscles. In higher organisms a mechanism develops connecting, with increasing delicacy, the sensory nerves, affected by changes in the environment, and the motor nerves controlling movements of muscles.

The result of such development is to enable a creature to vary its movements, its "behavior," in accordance with minute differences in the external changes which affect its nerves. It can adjust its reactions. The greater part of the mechanism for adjustment is located in the brain. Lower organisms possess mere nodes or knots where different sensory and motor nerves meet. From such rudiments a brain begins to develop higher up the scale. A complex web of paths grows up to connect the

---

[1] A distinction ought to be made between instincts and reflex actions; but that would involve subtleties irrelevant to our immediate argument.

various sensory nerves and to transmit impulses affecting them to the appropriate motor nerves. Sensations, which must at first have been nothing but fleeting impressions, could thus be permanently connected with one another and with movements, and so "remembered."

At last, instead of a couple of very simple movements, made indiscriminately to any change in its surroundings, the mammal can make different responses, appropriate to a very wide variety of external things and conditions affecting it. It is thus enabled to cope successfully with a greater diversity of circumstances. It can obtain its food more regularly and certainly, avoid its enemies more successfully, and propagate its kind more economically. The development of a nervous system and a brain made life possible under more varied conditions. And as conditions are constantly changing, such adaptability manifestly facilitated survival and multiplication.

Man appears very late in the geological record. No fossil skelton worth of the name of "man" is older than the last volume but one of the earth's history, the volume labelled "Pleistocene." Even then fossil remains are exceptionally rare till the concluding chapters, and fossil "men" of lower pleistocene age can be counted on the fingers. Whereas today all men belong to one species, *Homo sapiens,* and can all interbreed freely, the earlier pleistocene "men" belong to several distinct species. Some, indeed, diverge in bodily structure so widely from ourselves that anthropologists are inclined to assign them to distinct genera. The early members of the human family in question, the fossil hominids that are often termed paleanthropic, were not our direct evolutionary ancestors; in the pedigree of *Homo sapiens* they represent side branches from the main stem. And yet their bodies were better equipped than ours for certain physical functions, such as fighting. The canine teeth of *Eoanthropus* or Piltdown man, for instance, would be formidable weapons. But for the moment the distinctions within our family may be ignored.

Man is now, and was apparently even at his first appearance in the pleistocene, inadequately adapted for survival in any particular environment. His bodily equipment for coping with any special set of conditions is inferior to that of most animals. He has not, and probably never had, a furry coat like the polar bear's for keeping in the body's heat under cold conditions. His body is not particularly well adapted for escape, self-defense, or hunting. He is not, for instance, exceptionally fleet of foot, and would be left behind in a race with a hare or an ostrich. He has no protective coloring like the tiger or the snow leopard, nor bodily armor like the tortoise or the crab. He has no wings to offer escape and give him an advantage in spying out and pouncing upon prey. He lacks the beak and talons of the hawk and its keenness of vision. For catching his prey and defending himself, his muscular strength, teeth, and nails are incomparably inferior to those of the tiger.

In the comparatively short evolutionary history documented by fossil remains, man has not improved his inherited equipment by bodily changes detectable in his skeleton. Yet he has been able to adjust himself to a greater range of environments than almost any other creature, to multiply infinitely faster than any near relative among the higher mammals, and to beat the polar bear, the hare, the hawk, and the tiger at their special tricks. Through his control of fire and the skill to make clothes and houses, man can, and does, live and thrive from the Arctic Circle to the Equator. In the trains and cars he builds, man can outstrip the fleetest hare or ostrich. In airplanes he can mount higher than the eagle, and with telescopes see farther than the hawk. With firearms he can lay low animals that a tiger dare not tackle.

But fire, clothes, houses, trains, airplanes, telescopes and guns are not, we must repeat, part of man's body. He can leave them and lay them aside at will. They are not inherited in the biological sense, but the skill needed for their production and use is part of our social heritage, the result of a tradition accumulated over many generations, and transmitted, not in the blood, but through speech and writing.

Man's compensation for his relatively poor bodily endowment has been the possession of a large and complex brain, forming the center of an extensive and delicate nervous system. These permit a great variety of accurately controlled movements being adjusted exactly to the impulses received by keen organs of sense. It is only so that man has been enabled to make himself protections against climate and weather, arms and weapons of attack and defense that, because they can be adapted and adjusted, are really superior to furs, or teeth, or claws.

In a sense the possibility of making artifical substitutes for bodily defenses is a consequence of their absence. As long, for instance, as the bones of the brain-case have to support the powerful muscles needed to snap together a heavy jaw, like the chimpanzee's, and wield the fighting teeth it holds, the brain could get little room to expand; for the bone of the brain-case must be thick and solid. If the forelegs and forefeet have normally to carry the weight of the body, whether in walking or climbing, the fine and delicate movements of human fingers in grasping and making things would be impossible. At the same time, without hands to grasp food and handmade tools and weapons to secure food and repel attack, heavy jaws and fighting teeth such as are possessed by our ape relatives could scarcely be lightened or reduced in size. Thus the evolutionary changes which have contributed to the making of man are very intimately connected one with another and with the cultural changes which man himself has made. It is not surprising that in some early attempts at man they have progressed at different relative rates. Piltdown man (*Eoanthropus*), for example, possessed a brain-case comparable in size to our own, but preserved the heavy lower jaw and the projecting canines proper to an ape.

Man then is endowed by nature with a brain, big in comparison with his body, but this endowment is the condition enabling man to make his own culture. Other natural endowments are associated therewith and contribute towards the same result. Elliot Smith has brilliantly expounded the significance of "binocular vision" inherited from very remote and humble primate ancestors. Dorothy Davidson has given such a handy summary of the argument that recapitulation here is unnecessary. It means roughly that we and our evolutionary ancestors see with our two eyes a single picture where other mammals see two. Unobserved muscular sensations of the focusing requisite to unify the images received by the two eyes are an important factor in judging distance and seeing objects as solid (stereoscopically) instead of just flat. In man and higher primates the association of stereoscopic images with sensations of touch and muscular activity renders possible the perfect estimation of distances and depths. Without the latter the delicacy of hands and fingers would not suffice for tool making. It is the perfectly adjusted, but subconscious, co-operation of hand and eye that allows man to make tools from the roughest eolith to the most sensitive seismograph. Such co-operation is possible owing to the delicacy of the nervous system and the complexity of association paths in the big brain. But the nervous mechanism has become so established now that it works without attracting our attention.

Speech is made possible by similar endowments—a delicate and precise control by the motor nerves over the muscles of the tongue and the larynx, and an exact correlation of the muscular sensations due to movements of these organs with the sense of hearing. The establishment of the necessary connections between the several sensory and motor nerves concerned are effected in well-defined areas of the brain, especially those just above the ears. The impressions of rudimentary swellings of this part of the brain are visible on the brain-cases of very early attempts at men like *Pithecanthropus* (Java man), *Sinanthropus* (Pekin man), and *Eoanthropus* (Piltdown man). Even these early members of our family could "speak."

But in *Homo sapiens* these developments in the brain and nervous system go hand in hand with modifications in the arrangement for the attachment of the tongue muscles which are not found in other genera or species of "men" any more than in apes. As a result man is enabled to utter a much greater variety of sounds than any other animal.

The mechanism whereby visual, muscular, auditory, and other sensations and movements are so smoothly co-ordinated that we are normally unconscious of the separate elements, grows in the brain mostly after birth. But it can only do so because the bones of the infant's skull are comparatively soft and loosely knit, so that the brain can expand under them. But during this process the infant is quite helpless and easily injured. It is, in fact, wholly dependent upon its parents. The last statement would be true of the young of any mammal and of most birds. But in the case of human infants the condition of dependence lasts exceptionally long. The hardening and solidification of the human skull are retarded longer than in other animals, to allow of the greater expansion of the brain. At the same time, man is born with relatively few inherited instincts. There are, that is to say, comparatively few precise movements and responses which our nervous system is adjusted to promote automatically; man's instincts are for the most part very generalized tendencies.

Like any other young animal, the human child has therefore to "learn by experience" the appropriate response to a specific situation. It must find out the right movements to make in relation to any external event, and build up in its brain the appropriate connections between sensory and motor nerves. And, as in the case of young mammals, the process of learning is assisted by the example of the parents. Even a young rabbit will try to imitate its mother, and thus will learn how to choose its food and avoid dangers that actually threaten it. Such education is common to human and animal families. But in the case of man the process of education is transformed. The human parent can teach not only by example, but also by precept. The faculty of speech—that is, the physiological constitution of the human tongue, larynx, and nervous system—endows prolonged infancy with a unique importance.

On the one hand, prolonged infancy involves family life, the continued association of parents and children for several years. On the other hand, physiological conditions, as already indicated, allow man to emit a great variety of distinct articulate sounds. And a particular sound or group of sounds, a word, may be associated with a particular event or group of events in the external world. For instance, the sound or word "bear" may conjure up an image of a particular sort of dangerous but edible furry animal, together with readiness for the actions appropriate to an encounter with such. The first words may, of course, have in themselves to some extent suggested the object thus denoted. "Morepork" roughly resembles the cry of a certain Australian owl which is so named. But even in such a case there is a large element of convention in restricting the meaning and giving it precision. It is only the result of a tacit agreement, accepted by the early white settlers in Australia, that "morepork" has come to mean a sort of owl rather than, say, a gull. Generally, the conventional element is absolutely dominant. The extent to which sounds can of themselves suggest or imitate things is obviously very limited indeed. Really language is essentially a social product; words can have meanings and suggest things and events only in a society and by tacit agreement between its members. But the human family is a necessary social unit (not necessarily or probably the only original one).

Now an integral part of human education consists in teaching the child to speak. That means teaching it to utter in the recognized way certain sounds or words and to connect them with objects or events to which, it is agreed, the sounds should refer. Once this has been done, parents can, with the aid of language, instruct their offspring how to deal with situations which cannot conveniently be illustrated by actual concrete examples. The child need not wait till a bear attacks the family to learn how to avoid it. Instruction by example alone in such a case is liable to be fatal to some of the pupils. Language, however, enables the elders to forewarn the young of the danger while it is absent, and then demonstrate the appropriate course of action.

And, of course, speech is not only a vehicle by which parents can convey their own experiences to their children. It is also a means of communication between all members of a human group that speaks the same language, *i.e.*, observes common conventions as to the pronunciation of sounds and the meanings attached to them. One member can tell his fellows what he has seen and done, and all can compare their actions and reactions. Thus the experiences of the whole group can be pooled. What parents impart to their offspring is not simply the lessons of their own personal experience, but something much wider: the collective experience of the group. This is the tradition which is handed on from generation to generation, and the method of its transmission with the aid of language seems a peculiarity of the human family. It constitutes the last vital difference between organic evolution and human progress.

A member of an animal species inherits, in the form of instincts, the collective experience of that species. Dispositions to particular reactions in particular situations are innate in it just because they have furthered the survival of the species. Animals of its kind endowed with different instincts have been less successful, and so have been weeded out by natural selection. The establishment of hereditary instincts, beneficial to the species, may be regarded as a slow and rather wasteful process, comparable to that by which the mammoth acquired a hairy coat. The human child is taught rules and precepts for action that members of his group and their ancestors have found beneficial.

Now, at least theoretically, the body of traditional rules is not fixed and immutable. Fresh experiences may suggest to individuals additions and modifications. These, if found useful, will be communicated to, discussed, and tested by, the community as a whole, and eventually incorporated in the collective tradition. In reality, of course, the process is not nearly so simple as it sounds. Men cling passionately to old traditions and display intense reluctance to modify customary modes of behavior, as innovators at all times have found to their cost. The dead-weight of conservatism, largely a lazy and cowardly distaste for the strenuous and painful activity of real thinking, has undoubtedly retarded human progress even more in the past than today. Nevertheless, for the human species progress has consisted essentially in the improvement and adjustment of the social tradition, transmitted by precept and example.

The discoveries and inventions which to the archaeologist appear as the tangible proofs of progress are, after all, just concrete embodiments and expressions of innovations in social tradition. Each is rendered possible only by the accumulated experience handed on by tradition to the inventor; each means the addition to the tradition of new rules for action and behavior. The inventor of the telegraph had already at his disposal a body of traditional knowledge accumulated from prehistoric times onwards as to the production and transmission of electricity. So, much earlier, the inventor of the sailboat had already learned to make and navigate a dugout canoe and how to manufacture a mat or weave a cloth. At the same time, the new movements needed for working the telegraph and the sailboat will have to be taught as soon as the device becomes established. The appropriate rules will be added to the social tradition to be learned by subsequent generations.

Another implication of language in general and speech in particular here calls for remark. But in parenthesis it should first be noted that language is not confined to articulate sounds or their written reproduction. It includes also gestures, and ultimately picture writing. Gestures, like words, to some extent imitate and suggest the object intended, but they too are largely conventional; their meanings, like those of spoken sounds, have to be restricted by a tacit agreement between members of a society. You may indicate "bird" by flapping your arms, but only a convention could restrict the gesture to indicate a special sort of bird, or even "bird" as against say, "tree-shaken-by-wind." Gesture symbolism, probably very important in the infancy of human intercourse, has not lent itself to fruitful developments as has spoken language. We shall see later that picture writing suffers from the same disabilities as gesticulation.

The capacity for what is termed "abstract thinking"—probably a prerogative of the human species—depends largely upon language. To name a thing at all is an act of abstraction. The bear, on getting its name, is thereby picked out and isolated from the complex of sensations—trees, caves, twittering birds, etc.—with which it may be accompanied when actually confronting a man. And it is not only isolated, but also generalized. Actual bears are always individual; they may be big or little, black or brown, sleeping or climbing a tree. In the word "bear," such qualities, some of which would apply to any actual bear, are ignored, and attention is drawn to one or two common elements, characteristics that have been found to be common to a number of distinct individual animals. The latter are grouped together in an abstract class. In very primitive languages like those of the Australian aborigines, anything so abstract or general as bear or kangaroo would lack a name. There would be different and unrelated words for "male kangaroo," "female kangaroo," "young kangaroo," "kangaroo jumping," and so on.

Some degree of abstraction is, however, a feature of any language. But having thus abstracted the idea of bear from its concrete actual surroundings and stripped it of many particular attributes, you may combine the idea with other similarly abstracted ideas or endow it with attributes, though you have never encountered a bear in such surroundings or with such attributes. You may, for example, endow your bear with speech, or describe him playing a musical instrument. You can play with your words, and that play may contribute to mythology and magic. It may also lead to inventions if the things you are talking or thinking about can be actually made and tried. Talk of winged men certainly preceded by a long time the invention of a workable flying machine.

Combinations, such as those just described, can, of course, be made without the use of words, of sounds standing for things. Visual images (or mental pictures) will do instead. Such actually play a large part in the thinking of mechanical inventors. Still, in the beginnings of human thinking visual images may have played a less important part than might be expected. Thinking is a sort of action, and with many persons (including the writer) the power of forming mental pictures is limited by their capacity to draw or make models of the thing imagined. It was a long time before man learned to draw or model, but, as soon as he became man, he could make articulate sounds.

Be that as it may, words and mental images of sounds or of the muscular movements required for uttering them can be used for functions to which visual images are inapplicable. Words can stand for abstractions—electricity, force, justice— which cannot possibly be represented by any visual picture. For thinking of this high degree of abstraction spoken (or written) language would seem almost indispensable. Much of the thinking embodied in this book is of such a kind. Let the reader try to imagine this page translated into a series of pictures or imitative gestures. He will then grasp the part played by speech, one of man's physiological endowments, in the distinctively human activity of abstract thinking.

The evolution of man's body, of his physiological equipment, is studied by prehistoric anthropology, a branch of paleontology. Beyond the points already considered, its results have little bearing upon the subject of this book. Within our species improvements in the equipment which men make for themselves—i.e. in culture— have taken the place of bodily modifications. Prehistoric anthropology does not at present even dispose of concrete documents that illustrate accurately the evolutionary processes that must be regarded as necessary preliminaries to the intelligent creation of culture. None of the rare fossil "men" whose skeletons have survived from the earlier (pleistocene) Ice Ages can be classed among our direct ancestors. They do not represent stages in Nature's process of man-making, but abortive experiments—genera and species— that have died out.

The earliest skeletons of our own species belong to the closing phases of the last Ice Age and to the cultural periods termed, in France, Aurignacian, Solutrean, and Magdalenian. They are already so like our own skeletons that differences can be demonstrated only to expert anatomists. These late pleisto-cene men are already differentiated into several distinct vari-eties or races. There must obviously be a long evolutionary history behind them, but no reliably dated fossil illustrates it. And since the time when skeletons of *Homo sapiens* first ap-pear in the geological record, perhaps 25,000 years ago, men's bodily evolution has come virtually to a standstill, though his cultural progress was just beginning. "The physical difference between men of the Aurignacian and Magdalenian cultures on the one hand, and present-day men on the other, is negligible, while the cultural difference is immeasurable."[1] Progress in culture has, indeed, taken the place of further organic evolu-tion in the human family.

It is archaeology that studies this progress in culture. Its documents are the tools, weapons, and huts that men of the past made in order to secure food and shelter. They illustrate improving technical skill, accumulating knowledge, and ad-vancing organization for securing a livelihood. Obviously a finished tool, fashioned by human hands, is a good gauge of the manual dexterity of its maker. Rather less obviously is it the measure of the scientific knowledge of his period. Yet any tool does really reflect, albeit rather imperfectly, the science at the disposal of its makers. That is really self-evident in the case of a wireless valve[2] or an airplane. It is equally true of a bronze axe, but a word of explanation may be useful.

Archaeologists have divided the cultures of the past into Stone Ages (Old and New), Bronze Age, and Iron Age, on the basis of the material generally and by preference employed for cutting implements. Bronze axes and knives are tools distinc-tive of a Bronze Age as contrasted with stone ones, indicating an earlier Stone Age, or iron ones, marking the subsequent Iron Age. Now a great deal more science has to be applied in the manufacture of a bronze axe than in making a stone one. The former implies a quite considerable working knowledge of geology (to locate and identify the ores) and chemistry (to reduce them), as well as the mastery of complicated technical processes. A "Stone Age" folk, using exclusively stone imple-ments, presumably lacked that knowledge. So the criteria used by archaeologists to distinguish his several "ages" serve also as indexes to the state of science.

But when the tools, hut-foundations, and other archaeologi-cal remains of a given age and locality are considered not in isolation, but in their totality, they may reveal much more. They disclose not only the level of technical skill and science

[1] Leakey, *Adam's Ancestors*, p. 224.
[2] Radio tube.

attained, but also the manner in which their makers got their livelihood, their economy. And it is this economy which determines the multiplication of our species, and so its biological success. Studied from this angle, the old archaeological divisions assume a new significance. The archaeologist's ages correspond roughly to economic stages. Each new "age" is ushered in by an economic revolution of the same kind and having the same effect as the "Industrial Revolution" of the eighteenth century.

In the "Old Stone Age" (paleolithic period) men relied for a living entirely on hunting, fishing, and gathering wild berries, roots, slugs, and shellfish. Their numbers were restricted by the provision of food made for them by Nature, and seem actually to have been very small. In the "New Stone Age" (neolithic times) men control their own food supply by cultivating plants and breeding animals. Given favorable circumstances, a community can now produce more food than it needs to consume, and can increase its production to meet the requirements of an expanding population. A comparison of the number of burials from the Old Stone Age with that from the New in Europe and the Near East shows that, as a result of the neolithic revolution, the population had increased enormously. From the biological standpoint the new economy was a success; it had made possible a multiplication of our species.

The use of bronze always involves specialized industries, and generally organized trade. To secure bronze tools a community must produce a surplus of foodstuffs to support bodies of specialist miners, smelters, and smiths withdrawn from direct food production. Nearly always part of the surplus will have to be expended on the transportation of the ore from comparatively remote metalliferous mountains. Actually in the Near East the Bronze Age is characterized by populous cities wherein secondary industries and foreign trade are conducted on a considerable scale. A regular army of craftsmen, merchants, transport workers, and also officials, clerks, soldiers, and priests is supported by the surplus foodstuffs produced by cultivators, herdsmen, and hunters. The cities are incomparably larger and more populous than neolithic villages. A second revolution has occurred, and once more it has resulted in a multiplication of our species.

Particularly in Europe, probably also in tropical countries, the discovery of an economical process for producing iron in quantity that is the mark of the iron Age—had a similar result. Bronze had always been an expensive material because its constituents, copper and tin, are comparatively rare. Iron ores are widely distributed. As soon as they could be smelted economically, anyone could afford iron tools. But cheap iron tools allowed men to open up for cultivation fresh lands by clearing forests and draining clay soils that stone tools were impotent, bronze tools too rare, to tackle effectively. Once more population could and did expand, as the prehistory of Scotland or the early history of Norway dramatically demonstrates.

The cultural advances forming the basis of archaeological classification have then had the same sort of biological effect as mutations in organic evolution. In subsequent chapters the earlier advances will be considered in greater detail. It will be shown how economic revolutions reacted upon man's attitude to Nature and promoted the growth of institutions, science, and literature—in a word, of civilization as currently understood.

CHAPTER III

TIME SCALES

BEFORE proceeding to describe the content of the "ages" just defined, it is desirable to attempt to give some indication as to their duration. Without some such attempt no fair estimate of the tempo of human progress nor even of its reality is obtainable. But a very serious effort of the imagination is necessary. The drama of human history occupies a period measurable not in years so much as in centuries and even millennia. Geologists and archaeologists speak glibly of these great periods of time, as if they did not realize that they are of the same kind as periods we have ourselves lived through.

A year seems a long time to most of us; we look back upon it, crowded with more or less exciting events affecting our own lives, our town, our country, and the world at large. A decade, or ten years, can be visualized only slightly less vividly. We recall the last decade, filled with outstanding events, be it the records in fly-catching, murders, rapes, and divorces which alone are "featured" in the popular press, or personal experiences of equal historical significance, or even really important events like the discovery of heavy hydrogen or of the Royal Tombs of Ur. Our picture of longer periods is more attenuated. It is thirty-four years since the Boer War, which many of us can remember. In the interval we shall have witnessed all sort of events that have left a permanent impression on our minds. We shall recall the first flying-machines, the multiplication of automobiles, the beginnings of wireless communication with ocean liners, suffragettes, a world war, the Russian revolution, a general strike, and so on.

But thirty-four decades would take us right back to the spacious days of Queen Elizabeth. The period is ten times as long as that we have just been trying to remember. But we are not, as a rule, aware that it contained ten times as many events which to their witnesses were presumably just as important as those we have been recalling from our own lifetimes. Only a few, like the beheading of Charles I, America's declaration of independence, Waterloo, come at once to the mind of the average man. Some with an effort recall that during the period

Newton formulated his law of gravity, that electricity and
chemistry were first scientifically studied and applied, that
Linnaeus classified the kingdom of living matter, and Darwin
enunciated the doctrine of natural selection. But to realize that
each of those 340 years, each of those thirty-four decades, was
actually just as crowded with events as the year or the decade
we have just experienced ourselves is much harder. But the
effort should be made.

A greater strain is to follow; let us go back not thirty-four
decades, but ten times as far—thirty-four centuries. In Britain
we shall then have stepped back into a period when no written
records were kept, when tools were made exclusively of stone,
bone, and wood, iron or bronze being unknown or unobtain-
able, and when men spent more time on building the gigantic
tombs known as barrows than on necessities like houses and
roads. Three thousand four hundred years ago written records
were being kept only in Crete, Egypt, Hither Asia, and perhaps India and China. It is particularly hard to realize that in
those unstoried centuries events crowded upon the barbarian
inhabitants of Britain as thick and fast as last year, though no
rumor of those events reached the civilized Egyptians or
Babylonians. Yet to the actors the unrecorded (but not un-
remembered) events they assisted in or witnessed, such as the
erection of a barrow or the laying out of Stonehenge, were just
as exciting and memorable as those of the century now drawing to a close. For the beginning of humanity, however, we
must go back much further—not 3400 years nor even ten times
as long, but nearly 340,000.

In fact, in dealing with the remote beginnings of progress, a
year or even a century is too small a unit. We must be accustomed to count in millennia—thousands of years. Yet each
millennium was ten centuries or a hundred decades. And each
day, year, decade, or century was as crowded with events as the
last to be recorded in the newspapers, yearbooks, or histories.

To get accustomed to this method of reckoning, try putting
recorded history in terms of millennia (fractions are now conveniently disregarded). Half a millennium ago Columbus was
discovering America. A millennium back the Normans had
not yet landed in England, and Alfred sat upon the Saxon
throne. Two millennia take us beyond the bounds of British
history altogether. The British Isles were known to literate
people only by the tales of travelers and merchants, but Cicero
was making and writing speeches in Rome. Three millennia
ago, and we have to go outside Europe to find any written
records: Rome had not been founded, Greece was plunged in
a dark age of barbarian invasion, literature flourished only in

Egypt and Hither Asia. It is the time of Solomon in Palestine. Finally, five millennia take us back to the very beginnings of written history in Egypt and Babylonia. Beyond that there are no written historical records to lighten the darkness or to help us to realize the multiplicity of events happening every year. Yet civilization was already mature.

To obtain some idea of archaeological time let us consider the ruins of cities in Mesopotamia. The dead level of the alluvial plain between the Tigris and Euphrates is broken by *tells* or mounds, rising 60 feet or more above the surrounding ground. They are not natural hillocks, but each marks the site of an ancient settlement, and is composed entirely of the débris of ruined houses, temples, and palaces. In Iraq houses are still built of mud-bricks, not baked in a kiln, but simply dried in the sun. Such a house may with luck stand for a century. But eventually the rain will penetrate under the eaves or reach the foundations and disintegrate the plastic mud. The whole edifice will then flop down, a shapeless mass of mud or crumbling dust. The owner will not bother to cart away the débris. He will just level it down and build on the old site a new house with its foundations a couple of feet higher than the floor of the previous dwelling. The repetition of this process over successive centuries is responsible for the *tells* that break the monotony of the Mesopotamian plain.

At Warka, the biblical Erech, the Germans explored the center of such a *tell* by means of a deep shaft. The top of the shaft is the floor level of a temple that is itself prehistoric and about 5500 years old. From this level you may descend by a winding path cut in the walls of the shaft for a depth of over 60 feet! At every stage of the dizzy descent you can pick from the shaft's sides bits of pottery, mud bricks, or stone implements. The shaft is actually cutting through a mound, 60 feet high, composed entirely of the débris of successive settlements in which men had lived. The mound has grown up in the manner described above, but even the latest of the component settlements traversed in descending the shaft is more than five millennia old!

At the bottom we reach virgin soil—the soil of a marsh that had just emerged from the Persian Gulf. The lowest settlement represents the remote beginnings of human life in Southern Mesopotamia. But when we have descended to it, we are as far as ever from the beginning of human progress. To reach that we must plunge into geological time. But now figures become almost meaningless (and mainly guesswork). To grasp man's antiquity we must consider the vast changes in the earth's surface that our species had witnessed before ever the first settlers reached the site of Erech.

Large sheets of ice had spread over the greater part of Britain and Northern Europe, and glaciers from the Alps and the Pyrenees had filled the river valleys of France. In Britain the ice sheets had radiated from the Highlands and, sometimes joined with ice sheets from Scandinavia, had spread over the Lowlands and extended into Ireland and as far south as Cambridge. Round Edinburgh the ice is believed to have been over 1000 feet thick. It filled up the valleys and rode over the tops of the Pentland Hills. In France the Rhône glacier, that can be seen in the distance above the Lake of Geneva today, spread down the Rhône valley to Lyons.

The formation and spread of these glaciers and ice sheets must have taken a stupendous time. A glacier is a river of ice, not a frozen river. The extension of the Rhône glacier to Lyons does not mean that the Rhône was suddenly frozen over, but that the glacier flowed down from the high Alps to the level of Lyons. But a glacier flows very slowly: its motion is scarcely perceptible to the naked eye. The fastest rate of flow observed is only 100 feet per *day*, and often the flow is much slower. The great sheets of ice that flowed over the plains of East Anglia and North Germany did not move at anything like the above rate. In Greenland such ice sheets are now moving only a few inches a day; in Antarctica the rate of flow is about one-third of a mile per annum. How long must it have taken for the Rhône glacier to reach Lyons and the Scottish ice sheets to have spread to Suffolk!

And then the melting of the vast ice sheets must have been equally slow. A really big mass of ice takes a lot of fusing. An iceberg in midsummer can float south of New York. But, huge though it be, such a detached island of ice is immeasurably smaller and more fusible than the vast ice sheets and glaciers under consideration. Their melting must have been so gradual that the difference in the position of the ice edge between one summer and the next can hardly have been perceptible to contemporary men.

Yet humanity witnessed the advance and the disappearance of the ice sheets over Europe long before history began. Not only so. Many geologists believe that there were four distinct Ice Ages or glaciations during the pleistocene epoch. Four times glaciers and ice sheets would have spread slowly over Europe, and four times they would have imperceptibly melted away or dried up. And between each glacial episode there would have been a warm temperate interglacial epoch of uncertain duration. "Men" were living in Europe and elsewhere throughout these gradual changes. A consideration of their gradualness and vastness is a better guide to the length of prehistoric time than any piling up of monstrous numbers.

During the Ice Ages other equally slow changes were in progress, and a reference to these may reinforce the lesson provided by glaciations. Great Britain, for instance, became attached by land-bridges to the Continent, and then separated again while men were living on her territories. The movements involved were as slow as those which are occurring unnoticed before our eyes today. It is notorious that the coast of England is being devoured by the sea. Occasionally the spectacular collapse of a piece of cliff near Brighton or the destruction of a promenade calls attention to this erosion. But on the whole the process is imperceptible. Even in half a century its effects are too small to be reflected in a map even on a scale as large as one inch to the mile. Equally gradual is the building up of land by the discharge of rivers forming deltas or silting up estuaries.

At the beginning of the pleistocene a great deal of East Anglia was under the sea. The so-called crags of Norfolk are sediments laid down in the shallow sea that covered the county at that time. Gradually the accumulation of such silts, coupled with equally gradual upheavals of the earth's crust, joined Britain to the Continent, and ultimately made dry land of the North Sea basin. The Thames then joined the Rhine as a tributary and flowed out over a vast plain into the Arctic Ocean north of the Dogger Bank. The re-submergence of this area had not been completed when the ice sheets disappeared. A land-bridge to England may have still existed when the pleistocene period ended, and the sinking that destroyed it is still in progress. Its progress is no more perceptible today than in the earlier stages and in the previous stages of elevation. That again should emphasize the stupendous duration of the pleistocene.

The foregoing remarks are intended to help the reader to gauge the lengths of time which may be denoted by the archaeologists' "ages." But now a warning must be inserted as to the meaning of such "ages." The Old Stone Age, the New Stone Age, the Bronze Age, and the Iron Age must not be mistaken for absolute periods of time like the epochs of the geologist. In any one locality—say Southern England or Egypt —each age does indeed really occupy a definite period of historical time. And in all regions the several ages follow one another in the same order. But they did not begin nor end simultaneously all over the world. It must not be imagined that at a given moment in the world's history a trumpet was blown in heaven, and every hunter from China to Peru thereupon

flung aside his weapons and traps and started planting wheat
or rice or maize and breeding pigs and sheep and turkeys.

On the contrary, the Old Stone Age, at least in the economic
sense given to the term on p. 35, lasts till today in Central
Australia and in Arctic America. The neolithic revolution had
initiated the New Stone Age in Egypt and Mesopotamia about
7000 years ago. In Britain or Germany its effects are first perceptible three and a half millennia later, say about 2500 B.C.
By the time the New Stone Age was established in Britain,
Egypt and Mesopotamia had been in the Bronze Age for
about a thousand years. The New Stone Age in Denmark
did not end before 1500 B.C. In New Zealand it had not ended
when Captain Cook landed; the Maori were still using polished
stone tools and practicing a neolithic economy when England
was in the throes of the Industrial Revolution. The Australians'
economy was then still "paleolithic."

It is just as important to remember the relative character
of archaeological "ages" as it is to grasp the great lengths of
time they may denote in certain areas. The Old Stone Age
was indeed so enormously long that it may almost be treated
as a universal period, equivalent to the geologists' pleistocene.
But in considering its end the time lag between different areas
is of crucial importance. The equivalence between pleistocene
and paleolithic is preserved by many archaeologists through
the insertion of a Mesolithic Age, to which are assigned some
post-glacial archaeological remains from countries, like Britain
and Northwestern Europe in general, which were only affected
by the neolithic revolution long after the end of the Ice Age.
To the mesolithic would then be assigned those remains that
are later than the geological pleistocene but older than the
beginnings of the New Stone Age locally. Since economically
the Mesolithic Age was a mere continuance of the Old Stone
Age mode of life, it has seemed needless in this book to
complicate the picture with a Mesolithic. Provided the reader's
mind is free of preconceptions, identifying "ages" with periods
of universal time, the treatment in the subsequent chapters
should not prove misleading.

Perhaps one final warning is desirable. Contemporary
savages have just been described as living in the Stone Age
today. They have not, in fact, progressed beyond a Stone Age
economy. That does not justify the assumption that Stone
Age men, living in Europe or the Near East 6000 or 20,000
years ago, observed the same sort of social and ritual rules,
entertained the same beliefs, or organized their family rela-
tionships along the same lines as modern peoples on a comparable level of economic development. It is true that the

Bushmen of South Africa, the Eskimos of Arctic America, and the Arunta in Central Australia get their food in the same sort of way as the men of the Ice Age in Europe. Their material equipment and even their art are sometimes strikingly like those left by Aurignacians or Magdalenians in glacial Europe. A study of the processes by which these modern savages make tools and of how they use them is an illuminating and probably reliable guide to the techniques and skills of our remote ancestors. An examination of the habits of the Eskimos is the best way of seeing how men can live under conditions such as ruled in Europe in the Ice Ages.

But we may be invited to go further and seek in savages' institutions, rituals, and beliefs the living counterpart of that aspect of prehistoric life and culture upon which archaeology is inevitably silent. The prospect is alluring, but the reader must not be misled by its enticements. Because the economic life and the material culture of these tribes have been "arrested" at a stage of development Europeans passed through some 10,000 years ago, does it follow that their mental development stopped dead at the same point?

The Arunta are satisfied with a very simple equipment that does, however, suffice to provide them with food and shelter in the Australian environment. Their material equipment is very much on the same technical level as, and in some points identical with, that of Old Stone Age hunters in Europe and North Africa. But the Arunta observe (to us) most complicated rules for the regulation of marriage and reckoning of kinship, they perform very elaborate and sometimes very painful ceremonies for magico-religious ends, they profess a medley of puzzling and incoherent beliefs about totems, animals, ancestors, and spirits. It would surely be rash to regard such social rules, ceremonies, and beliefs as an uncontaminated heritage from a "primitive condition of man."

Why should we attribute such ideas and practices to Stone Age men of 20,000 years ago? Why assume that, when the Arunta had created a material culture adapted to their environment, they at once stopped thinking altogether? They may have gone on thinking just as much as our own cultural ancestors, although their thoughts followed different lines and did not lead them to the same practical results, applied sciences, and arithmetic, but along what we regard as blind alleys of superstition. Moreover, they may have been exposed to influences from the great civilizations the commerce of which has been percolating to the uttermost corners of the earth for the last 5000 years. Some ethnographers at least claim to recognize in the material culture, social organization, and religion of the Australians, elements and ideas taken over and adapted from more advanced peoples in the Old World.

Other very primitive tribes seem to have lost elements of culture that they once enjoyed. The Bushmen of South Africa would be an unfortunate stock that has been driven into poor and arid wastes by stronger peoples, like the Bantu. In their new and unfavorable environment, arts once practiced may have been neglected and forgotten. Finds from old refuse heaps, for instance, suggest that the Bushmen's ancestors once manufactured pottery which is no longer made. Social institutions and religious beliefs may have been disintegrated and distorted at the same time. Such a group is impoverished, not primitive.

The assumption that any savage tribe today is primitive in the sense that its culture faithfully reflects that of much more ancient men is gratuitous. We shall frequently invoke the ideas and practices of contemporary savages to illustrate how ancient peoples, known only to archaeology, may have done things or interpreted them. But save in so far as such modern practice and belief are used as a mere gloss or commentary on actually observed ancient objects, constructions, or operations, the usage is illegitimate. The thoughts and beliefs of prehistoric men have perished irrevocably save in so far as they were expressed in action the results of which were durable and can be recovered by the archaeologist's spade.

CHAPTER IV

FOOD GATHERERS

MAN'S emergence on the earth is indicated to the archaeologist by the tools he made. Man needs tools to supplement the deficiencies of his physiological equipment for securing food and shelter (p. 20). He is enabled to make them by the delicate correlation of hand and eye rendered possible by the constitution of his brain and nervous system (p. 28). The first tools would presumably be bits of wood, bone, or stone, very slightly sharpened or accommodated to the hand by breaking or chipping. In so far as they were made of wood, they will have perished. The earliest stone tools will normally be indistinguishable from the products of natural fracture (stones splintered by frost or heat or shattered by jostling in a river gravel). However, even from times prior to the first Ice Age, archaeologists have recognized pieces of flint that appear to be intelligently chipped, as if to adapt them to serve as knives, choppers, and scrapers. The human workmanship of such "eoliths" is indeed still disputed, but is admitted by the majority of authorities.

In quite early pleistocene times there were certainly "men" manufacturing unmistakable implements of stone and also controlling fire. Conclusive evidence has been obtained from the cave of Choukou-tien near Pekin (Pei-ping). There, together with the fossilized remains of "Pekin man" and of extinct animals, were found very crudely fashioned flakes of quartzite and other stones, and also bones that had indubitably been subjected to the action of fire. Superior tools have been found in geological deposits of the same age in East Anglia and elsewhere, but not definitely associated with "human" skeletons. Little is to be learned from tools of this sort; they reveal that some manlike creature was adapting stones to his rudimentary needs, but little more. What the tools were made for can only be guessed. Hides and skins take a lot of "dressing," and contemporary savages employ a variety of tools in preparing them for service as coats or shelters. Some of the implements thus employed for scraping hides are very like early flints, and so archaeologists are rather fond of labeling rude implements "scrapers." The term implies that men were not only fashioning tools, but also using them to dress hides for clothing, but the correctness of this tacit inference is, of course, unproven.

Most probably the first tools served a multitude of purposes. Early man had gradually to learn by experience what stones were most suitable for the manufacture of tools and how to chip them correctly. Even flint—the best natural material— is very hard to manipulate successfully, as the reader may easily discover by hitting flint nodules against one another and trying to produce a "flake." In the course of making tools, the earliest communities had to build up a scientific tradition, noting and transmitting what were the best stones, where they were to be expected, and how they were to be handled. Only after he had mastered the technique of manufacture, could man successfully start making special tools for each individual operation. At first the best obtainable flake must serve indiscriminately as chopper, saw, borer, knife, or scraper. The demonstrated facts are the manufacture of tools and the control of fire.

The control of fire was presumably the first great step in man's emancipation from the bondage to his environment. Warmed by the embers, man could endure cold nights, and could thus penetrate into temperate and even arctic regions. The flames would give him light at night and allow him to explore the recesses of sheltering caves. Fire would scare away other wild beasts. By cooking, substances became edible that would be indigestible if eaten raw. Man is no longer restricted in his movements to a limited range of climates, and his activities need not be entirely determined by the sun's light.

But in mastery of fire man was controlling a mighty physical force and a conspicuous chemical change. For the first time in history a creature of Nature was directing one of the great forces of Nature. And the exercise of power must react upon the controller. The sight of the bright flame bursting forth when a dry bough was thrust into glowing embers, the transformation of the bough into fine ashes and smoke, must have stimulated man's rudimentary brain. What these phenomena suggested to him is unknowable. But in feeding and damping down the fire, in transporting and using it, man made a revolutionary departure from the behavior of other animals. He was asserting his humanity and making himself.

At first, of course, man just tamed and kept alight fires that had been produced by lightning or other natural agency. Even that presupposes some science—observation and comparison of experiences. Man had to learn what the effects of fire were, what it would "eat," and so on. And in tending and preserving the flames man kept adding to his store of knowledge. Sacred fires that must never be allowed to die out, like the fire of Vesta at Rome, were ritually tended by many ancient peoples and by modern savages. They are presumably survivals and reminiscences of a time when man had not yet learned to produce fire at will.

When that discovery was made is uncertain. Savage peoples produce fire by the spark from flint struck against iron pyrites or hematite, by the friction of two pieces of wood, or by the heat generated on compressing air in a tube of bamboo. The first device was being employed in Europe as early as the last Ice Age. Several modifications of the friction method (fire plow, fire drill, and so on) are current among savages in different parts of the modern world, and are mentioned in ancient literatures. Perhaps the variety of methods used for kindling fire indicates that the trick was discovered only relatively late in human history, when our species had already been widely scattered into isolated groups.

In any case, the discovery was one of first-class significance. Man could thereafter not only control but also initiate the puzzling process of burning, the mysterious power of heat. He became consciously a creator. The evocation of flame out of a pair of sticks or from flint, pyrites, and tinder looks very like making something out of nothing. When it was a less familiar event, it must have had a very exhilarating effect; you must have felt yourself a creator indeed. But of course man was a creator in shaping a piece of wood or stone into a tool. He was asserting a power over Nature and molding objects to his will.

Such are the only certain facts that emerge from a study of the remains actually left by early pleistocene and pre-pleistocene "men." What they lived on is unknown. It is assumed that the earliest men snared and hunted wild animals and birds, caught fishes and lizards, collected wild fruits, shellfish, and eggs, and dug for roots and grubs. It is also assumed, but with less confidence, that they made coats of skins. Some certainly took refuge in caves, others may have erected rude shelters of boughs. Success in hunting could only be attained by prolonged and accurate observation of the habits of game; the results must have been built up into a collective tradition of hunting lore. The distinction between nutritive and poisonous plants again had presumably to be learned by experience, and once more incorporated in a communal tradition.

Man must learn the right seasons for hunting the different

species of game or collecting the several kinds of eggs and
fruits. To do so successfully he must eventually decipher the
calendar of the heavens; he must observe the phases of the
moon and the risings of stars, and compare these observations
with the botanical and zoological ones already mentioned.
And, as noted, man had to discover by experiment the best
stones for making tools and where such occurred. For even
the earliest men success in life required a considerable body
of astronomical, botanical, geological, and zoological knowledge. In acquiring and transmitting this our forerunners were
laying the foundations of science.

It may equally well be inferred that men learned to co-
operate and act together in getting their livelihood. A creature
so weak and poorly endowed as man could not in isolation
successfully hunt the large or fierce animals that quite early
provided an important item in his diet. Some form of social
organization beyond the simple family (in the modern
European sense of that word) has to be postulated, but the
precise form is unknown.

And nothing material can be added to the picture till the
last Ice Age in Europe was approaching. In the interval we
can, indeed, discern improvements in the manufacture of
flint tools and regional divergences in the methods of working.
In some areas the toolmakers concentrated upon detaching
convenient flakes from the parent lump (technically termed
the core); the flakes were then trimmed up to serve as the
actual tools. The procedure gives what archaeologists term a
flake industry. Elsewhere attention was devoted rather to
reducing the core itself to a handy shape by chipping bits off
it; in this case the trimmed core becomes the actual tool, and
an assemblage of such is termed a core industry.

The distinction seems due to divergent traditions in flint-
work followed by two different groups of "men." In a general
way it seems that flake industries were confined to the northern
part of the Old World—to the zone north of the great mountain spine marked by the Alps, Balkans, Caucasus, Hindu
Kush, and Himalayas. Such skeletons as have been found associated with flake industries belong to creatures specifically
or even generically different from ourselves or from any possible ancestor of ours. Core industries have been found in
Southern India, in Syria and Palestine, all over Africa, in
Spain, France, and England. Their makers may have belonged
to the species *Homo sapiens* or to forms ancestral to him, but
positive evidence is still lacking in 1941. During Ice Ages the
flake people tended to spill over from their proper domain,
which was getting frozen over, into England and France and

Syria, and ultimately even into Africa. Core industries during the same Ice Ages withdrew southward only to spread north again when genial conditions returned. As a result of these displacements of peoples, communities following different industrial traditions came to live side by side. There are hints of a blending of the two traditions, though intercourse between creatures so different as, say, *Sinanthropos* and *Homo sapiens* is difficult to conceive.

The last few pages summarize four-fifths of human history —say on a modest estimate 200,000 years! From that vast period survive nine or ten imperfect skeletons and innumerable tools. The cellars of English and French museums are crammed with implements collected from the gravels of the Thames, the Seine, and other rivers, and in South Africa it is easy to pick up a cartload of tools on the surface at many sites. But the stupendous numbers of the earlier pleistocene tools need not betoken a large population. On the contrary, a single individual might make and lose three or four tools every day, and 200,000 years were available for making those we now collect! In early to middle pleistocene times the human family was probably a numerically small group, comparable in size to that of contemporary manlike apes.

First about 50,000 years ago does it become possible to add any significant details to the foregoing vague sketch. As the last Ice Age was approaching, groups of "men" who used to be termed Mousterians became prominent in Europe. As they habitually lived in caves to escape the intense cold, more details are known of their lives than of those of earlier groups. Industrially the Mousterians were adherents of the flake tradition, though some learned to make core implements too. Physically they belonged to the Neanderthal species, now extinct. They walked with a shuffling gait and could not hold their heads erect. Their jaws were chinless, and a huge bony ridge over the eyes and a retreating forehead gave their faces a bestial look. They could talk sufficiently to organize their cooperative hunting expeditions, but, judging from the attachments for the tongue muscles, their speech must have been very halting.

Economically the Mousterians were hunters and had specialized in trapping huge arctic mammals—the mammoth and the woolly rhinoceros, whose carcasses they would drag to the mouth of their cave and there cut up. Naturally such big beasts cannot have been pursued by individuals or small families; mammoth hunting is a trade for some larger social unit co-operating for economic ends.

Historically the most notable fact about the Mousterians

is the care they devoted to the disposal of the dead. More than
a dozen Neanderthal skeletons have been found in France,
ritually buried in the caves where their group lived. Generally
attempts had been made to protect the body. At La Chapelle
aux Saints several skeletons lay each in a shallow grave dug
in the cave floor. The head sometimes rests on a stone pillow,
with stones above and around it to relieve the pressure of the
earth. In one instance the head had been severed from the
trunk before interment and placed in the grave apart. Not only
were the dead carefully interred: their graves were placed
near the hearths, as if to warm their occupants. The departed
was provided with tools and joints of meat.

All this ceremonial bears witness to the activity of human
thought in unexpected and uneconomic directions. Faced with
the terrifying fact of death, their primitive emotions shocked
by its ravages, the bestial-looking Mousterians had been roused
to imaginative thinking. They would not believe in the complete cessation of earthly life, but dimly imagined some sort
of continuance thereof in which the dead would still need
material food and implements. The pathetic and futile
tendance of the dead, thus early attested, is destined to become
a rooted habit of human behavior which inspired such architectural wonders as the Pyramids and the Taj Mahal.

Perhaps a further inference may be hazarded from the dis-
position of the graves near to hearths. Did the Mousterians
somehow hope by the warmth of the fire to restore to the
departed a quality the loss of which they recognized as symp-
tomatic of death? If so they were already practicing magic
and misapplying science. They would have correctly observed
an association between life and warmth. They might infer that
warmth was a cause of life: death would be due to a deficiency
of warmth. In that case to remedy the deficiency might restore
life. In this way good logical reasons could be assigned for the
Mousterian and later burial practices. Their error would be
that, having made the experiment repeatedly, they refused to
admit its failure: for Mousterians and their successors of our
own species went on kindling fires in graves down to comparatively recent times.

It cannot be proved that the Mousterians were actuated by
the motives here suggested, and it is certainly not pretended
that they or any modern votary of magic formulated their
reasons in the terms just mentioned. The argument here outlined is that which would have led a modern scientist to do
what the Mousterian did. But the scientist would have done it
as an experiment once or twice to see if it had the desired
result. The Mousterian did it as an act of faith, and that is

what distinguishes a magical operation from a scientific experiment. In judging its results, negative instances, *i.e.* failures, are simply ignored. Or rather objective judgment gives place to hope and fear. The fervor of man's faith in magic remedies is proportionate to his sense of helplessness in the face of a crisis like death. Feeling very helpless, he just dare not let that hope go. And just in so far as Nature seems alien and unknown is man afraid to omit anything that might help him in that menacing environment.

At the same time, magic offers a short cut to power. The sort of argument I have quoted offers an apparently logical account of, say, life. But it has been reached without any penetrating and searching analysis. Hating thought, man accepts the explanation that lies nearest at hand and desperately clings to it.

A few millennia later the glacial climate of Europe improved slightly for a time. During this warmer interval men of our own species first appear positively in the archaeological record in Europe, North Africa, and Hither Asia. Neanderthal "man" abruptly disappears; his place is taken by modern men, whose bodies would hardly provoke comment in a mortuary today. Physically at least four distinct varieties or races can be recognized in Europe alone, with statuettes from Siberia show the peculiar forms of hair distinctive of the three major divisions of our species. Archaeologically the products of these modern men, termed Upper Paleolithic industries, fall into several cultural groups, each distinguished by its own peculiar traditions in flint-work, art, and so on. No exact correlation can, however, be established between the cultural and the racial groups.

All Upper Paleolithic groups are far better equipped for dealing with the environment than any previously encountered. They have learnt to make a variety of distinct tools adapted to particular uses; they even make tools for making tools. They work bone and ivory as skilfully as flint; they have even invented simple mechanical devices like the bow and the spear-thrower to supplement human muscular power in hurling weapons. And, of course, such an array of new tools indicates not only increased technical skill, but also greater accumulations of knowledge and wider applications of science. A brief reference to the Predmostians of East and Central Europe and to the Aurignacians and Magdalenians in France should suffice to illustrate these points.

Despite the intense cold, the environment in Europe was eminently favorable for hunters equipped to meet it. The plains of Russia and Central Europe were open tundras or steppes. Every summer bitter winds blowing off the glaciers and ice sheets covered these plains with a layer of fine dust (löss), through which young herbage sprouted each spring. Vast herds of mammoth, reindeer, bison, and wild horse ranged over the plains, browsing on the grass. Every year the herds migrated from summer pastures in Russia and Siberia

FIG. 3.—ARCHERS AND ARROWS IN A STONE AGE PAINTING FROM SOUTHEAST SPAIN.

to winter grazing in the Danube valley or on the Pontic steppe and back again.

The Předmostian hunters pitched their camps along passes between ice-capped mountains that such herds must traverse and where tongues projecting from the northern ice sheet restricted the beasts' movements. The camp sites are still marked by immense middens discovered under the löss at Mezine near Kiev, at Předmost near Prerau in Moravia, at Willendorf in Lower Austria, and elsewhere. The size of the bone heaps— remains of over 1000 mammoths were recognized at Předmost

—attests the hunters' success in procuring mammoth meat.
There was food enough for a vigorous population. But the
meat could only be obtained by the effective co-operation of
a substantial number of individuals and by detailed knowledge of the habits of the herds; the clever location of the
camp sites proves the application of such knowledge. Russian
excavators have shown that the hunters erected substantial
half-subterranean houses to live in.

Even more favorable conditions prevailed in Central France.
The limestone plateaus were steppes on which browsed mammoths, reindeer, bisons, musk oxen, horses, and other edible
animals. Salmon ran every year in the waters of the Dordogne,
the Vezère, and other rivers as abundantly as in British
Columbia today. The walls of the valleys are honeycombed
with caves offering convenient habitations. By exploiting this
environment intelligently, the Aurignacians and their successors, the Magdalenians, multiplied and created a rich
culture. They were no more homeless nomads than were the
Kwakiutl of British Columbia who last century, despite a
"paleolithic" economy, lived in substantial and even ornate
wooden houses grouped in permanent villages. Such prosperity
is a warning against underrating the possibilities of food-
gathering as a livelihood.

The deep Upper Paleolithic deposits in the caves, the masses
of tools that can be collected, suggest an increased population.
The number of Upper Paleolithic skeletons found in France
alone exceeds that of all earlier skeletons put together. Yet the
period over which they must be distributed is not one-
twentieth of that to which the latter belong. Nevertheless, the
number of Upper Paleolithic skeletons is not one-hundredth
of that attributed to the neolithic period in France, which did
not last a fifth of the time assigned to the Aurignacian and
Magdalenian phases. Intelligent exploitation of an eminently
favorable environment enabled the Aurignacian hunters to
multiply beyond all former inhabitants of Western Europe,
but their numbers fell far short of those attained by their
successors after the neolithic revolution.

With game so abundant as to ensure security and even
leisure, the Aurignacians[1] were enabled to build up on traditions inherited from unknown ancestors a varied cultural life.
On the material side its most striking traits are the possession
of engines—the spear-thrower and the bow. The bow is, indeed, not certainly attested among the French Aurignacians,

[1] It is now agreed that what used to be called the Aurignacian culture is
really three distinct cultures. For the purposes of this book this newly recognized complexity may be conveniently ignored.

but was used by contemporary but distinct people in East
Spain. It is perhaps the first engine man devised. The motive
power is, indeed, just human muscular energy, but in the ten-
sion of the bow energy gradually expended in bending it is
accumulated so as to be released all at once and concentrated in dispatching the arrow. The spear-thrower ingeniously
augments the energy man's arm can impart to a missile on the
principle of the lever. It may have been invented first in the
Magdalenian phase, and is still employed by the Australian
aborigines and by the Eskimos. The Magdalenians had, moreover, learned to catch fish both with hook and line and with
harpoons furnished with detachable heads.

These peoples must have lived in communities large enough
to hunt successfully big game like mammoth and bison. How
they were organized is, of course, unknown. Economically
each group was self-sufficient. But self-sufficiency does not
spell isolation; shells brought from the Mediterranean have
been found in the caves of Central France. Presumably they
were brought thither by some rudimentary form of trade.
Still, shells, though valued for supposed magical virtues, are
luxuries, not necessities. The trade they denote played no
essential part in the group's economy. That was based upon
hunting and collecting and, at least by Magdalenian times, on
fishing. No evidence for the production of food by the cultivation of plants and breeding of animals has yet come to light
in France or anywhere else at this period. Steps for the conservation of game by the observance of close seasons may be
inferred from the customs of contemporary savages. Nevertheless, the woolly rhinoceros became extinct during Aurignacian
times, the mammoth towards the close of the Magdalenian,
perhaps through too-successful hunting.

The most surprising and celebrated aspect of Upper Paleolithic cultures is the artistic activity of the hunters. They carved
figures in the round in stone or ivory, modeled animals in clay,
decorated weapons with representations and formal designs,
executed bas-reliefs on the rock walls of cave shelters, and engraved or painted scenes on the ceilings of caverns. In many instances their products are in themselves of high artistic merit.
Great modern artists, like the late Roger Fry, admire cave-
paintings not as curiosities, but as masterpieces. The actual development of the power of drawing can be studied in the
French caves. The oldest representations, assigned to the Aurignacian phase, are just profile outlines, traced with the
finger in mud, scratched with a flint on the rock, or sketched
in charcoal; no attempt has been made at perspective or to

fill in details. In Magdalenian times the artist learned by shading to suggest depth, and even achieved a certain amount of perspective. Now remember we see things in three dimensions; it is difficult to represent them effectively in two. We have inherited a technique of doing this and of reinterpreting two-dimensional drawings. From childhood we become familiar with flat pictures, and learn to recognize in them solid objects. Some of us can be taught to reverse the process and to reproduce depth and distance on a sheet of paper. The Aurignacians or some earlier artistic ancestors had no picture-books. They had themselves to discover the technique of depicting solids on a flat surface correctly and to establish the tradition. And incidentally drawing is as important to modern science as is writing.

Yet the paleolithic sculptures and drawings are not merely expressions of a mysterious "artistic impulse." The artist, indeed, surely enjoyed executing them, but he did not do it just to secure that joy, but for a serious economic motive. That is most obviously true in the case of the cave paintings and engravings. The pictures are generally situated in the deep recesses of limestone caves whither no daylight can penetrate. No families have ever lived in these fastnesses; they are often very difficult of access. And in executing the drawings the artist had often to adopt most uncomfortable attitudes, lying on his back or standing on a comrade's shoulders in a narrow crevice. Of course he had to work by a dim artificial light: the stone lamps have actually been found; fat may be assumed as the fuel, with moss for a wick. The pictures are almost exclusively very faithful portraits of individual animals. The artist has evidently been at great pains to make his representation lifelike; we even possess trial pieces, rough sketches on loose blocks of stone, made in preparation for the actual masterpiece on the cave wall.

All these considerations show that cave art had a magic purpose. An artistic production is, after all, an act of creation. The artist scratches upon the blank wall, and lo, there is a bison where formerly there had been none! To the logic of pre-scientific minds such a creation must have a counterpart in the outside world that could be tasted as well as seen. As surely as the artist drew a bison in the dark cavern, so surely would there be a living bison in the steppes outside for his fellows to kill and eat. To make sure of success, the artist occasionally (but rarely) drew his bison transfixed by a dart, as he desired to see it.

Aurignacian and Magdalenian art was therefore practical in

its aim, and designed to ensure a supply of those animals on which the tribe depended for its food. So the Australian Arunta and other modern food-gatherers perform dances and other ceremonies intended to promote the multiplication of emus and witchetty grubs and other edible animals or plants. If they could understand its implications, they would indignantly repudiate the title "food-gatherers" used to contrast them with the "food-producing" Papuan who cultivates yams. "Our magic rites," an Arunta would say, "are just as necessary and efficacious in keeping up the supply of emus and grubs, as the digging and weeding done by wretched cultivators."

The picture were doubtless connected with other magical ceremonies. In a scarcely accessible niche in the cave of Montespan the mud still preserves the marks left by the buttocks of youths who had squatted there before a magic picture in Magdalenian times. That sounds quite like the initiation ceremonies practiced by savage tribes today.

In any case, the artists must have been trained specialists. At Limeuil in the Dordogne a number of trial pieces executed on pebbles have been collected. They may be the copybooks of an art school; on some pieces corrections, as if by a master's hand, have been noticed. The artist-magicians were experts, specially trained for their task. As such they must have enjoyed respect, and even authority, in whatever social organization then existed. But they can hardly have been specialists in the sense of being exempted from participation in the active food-quest of the group; the lifelike representation of animals in all sorts of natural attitudes could only be achieved by men who had closely studied the beasts in their native haunts as a hunter must.

Other products of paleolithic art may be regarded as magic too, but in rather different ways. From Predmostian and more rarely from Aurignacian stations come small figurines of women, carved out of stone or ivory. Normally the bodies are excessively fat and the sexual features exaggerated, but the face is left almost blank. It is assumed that such were fertility charms. The generative powers of women would inhere in them, and through them be canalized to provide food for the tribe by ensuring the fertility of game and vegetation.

Finally, Upper Paleolithic art is valuable as providing a rough index of the zoological knowledge possessed by men of that age. The faithfulness of their delineation illustrates the accuracy of their observations upon those animals that provided their food. From the pictures it is still possible to distinguish the several species intended, even in the case of fishes and deer. Magdalenians evidently recognized the same species as a modern zoologist. They understood something of animal physiology. At least they grasped the importance of the heart; a wounded bison is depicted with his heart exposed and transfixed by a dart.

On the other hand, Magdalenian and Aurignacian art is excessively concrete. The drawings are portraits of individual animals in individual attitudes; there is nothing generalized about them. This need not mean that Magdalenians were incapable of abstract thinking (as defined on p. 32). It does probably indicate that their thinking was habitually as concrete as possible. In East Spain pictures, belonging to a rather later period but to a distinct social tradition, are much less lifelike and individual; they are impressionistic, and suggest deer and man much more than this deer or that man. In fact, after the Ice Age they lead on to a series of quite conventional representations. The artist no longer tries to portray, or even to suggest, an individual living stag; he is content with the fewest possible strokes to indicate the essential attributes by which a stag may be recognized. On the one hand, he has found out that a shorthand sketch is just as effective as a life portrait in multiplying edible stags in the real world. On the other hand, he has habituated himself to abstract thinking. He has grasped the idea of stag as contrasted with this or that stag, and has symbolized it in the most generalized form, omitting all the individual peculiarities that distinguish one stag from another or the same stag at different times.

The above account will indicate, however imperfectly, the extent of human progress during the Old Stone Age, the pleistocene period of geology. The Magdalenian culture of France is the most brilliant achievement of that long episode so far known to archaeology. The account here given should afford a glimpse of the prosperity, refinement, and density of population attainable by a hunting and collecting economy. It will indicate the wide variety of modes of life comprised under the general term "food-gathering," and serve as a warning against attaching an unduly derogatory sense thereto.

Nevertheless it was not among the Magdalenians of Europe that the neolithic revolution was initiated and the new economy created. The Magdalenians owed their prosperity to a successful adjustment to a special environment. When, with the passing of the last Ice Age, forest invaded the former steppes and tundra and ousted the herds of mammoth, bison, horse, and reindeer from France, the culture, based upon the hunting of these animals, decayed. Other peoples, who have left no such brilliant memorials behind them, created the new food-producing economy. It is, in fact, conceivable that, even in the days of the Aurignacian and Magdalenian hunters of Europe, tribes in other continents had begun cultivating plants and breeding animals. Professor Menghin and others have been led to infer this. But up to date no positive evidence has been adduced to confirm the inference. On the available evidence, during the Old Stone Age, *i.e.* the pleistocene era, gathering and hunting were the sole methods practiced by man in securing a livelihood.

CHAPTER V

THE NEOLITHIC REVOLUTION

THROUGHOUT the vast eras of the Ice Ages man had made no fundamental change in his attitude to external Nature. He had remained content to take what he could get, though he had vastly improved his methods of getting and had learned discrimination in what he took. Soon after the end of the Ice Age man's attitude (or rather that of a few communities) to his environment underwent a radical change fraught with revolutionary consequences for the whole species. In absolute figures the era since the Ice Age is a trifling fraction of the total time during which men or manlike creatures have been active on the earth. Fifteen thousand years is a generous estimate of the post-glacial period, as against a conservative figure of 250,000 years for the preceding era. Yet in the last twentieth of his history man has begun to control Nature, or has at least succeeded in controlling her by co-operating with her.

The steps by which man's control was made effective have been gradual, their effects cumulative. But among them we may distinguish some which, judged by the standards explained in Chapter I, stand out as revolutions. The first revolution that transformed human economy gave man control over his own food supply. Man began to plant, cultivate, and improve by selection edible grasses, roots, and trees. And he succeeded in taming and firmly attaching to his person certain species of animal in return for the fodder he was able to offer, the protection he could afford, and the forethought he could exercise. The two steps are closely related. Many authorities now hold that cultivation is everywhere older than stock-breeding. Others, notably the German historical school, believe that, while some human groups were beginning to cultivate plants, other groups were domesticating animals. Very few still contend that a stage of pastoralism universally preceded cultivation. For purposes of exposition we shall here adopt the first theory. Even today many tribes of cultivators survive who possess no domestic animals. In Central Europe and Western China, where mixed farming has been for centuries the prevailing economy, the oldest peasants revealed by the archaeologist's spade relied very little, if at all, on domestic animals, but lived on agricultural produce and perhaps a little game.

Quite a large variety of plants are capable of providing a staple diet under cultivation. Rice, wheat, barley, millet, maize, yams, sweet potatoes, respectively support considerable populations even today. But in the civilizations which have contributed most directly and most generously to the building up of the cultural heritage we enjoy, wheat and barley lie at the foundations of the economy. These two cereals offer, in fact, exceptional advantages. The food they yield is highly nutritious, the grains can easily be stored, the return is relatively high, and, above all, the labor involved in cultivation is not too absorbing. The preparation of the fields and sowing certainly demand a considerable effort; some weeding and watching are requisite while the crop is ripening; harvest demands intensive exertion by the whole community. But these efforts are seasonal. Before and after sowing come intervals in which the fields need practically no attention. The grain grower enjoys substantial spells of leisure, during which he can devote himself to other occupations. The rice grower, on the other hand, enjoys no such respite. His toil need perhaps never be so intensive as that demanded by the grain harvest, but it is more continuous.

As the historic civilizations of the Mediterranean basin, Hither Asia, and India were built upon cereals, we shall confine our attention to the economies based upon wheat and barley. The histories of these have been much more extensively studied than those of other cultivated plants, and may be briefly indicated.

Both wheats and barleys are domesticated forms of wild grasses. But in each case cultivation, the deliberate selection for seed purposes of the best plants, and conscious or accidental crossings of varieties have produced grains far larger and more nutritive than any wild grass-seeds. Two wild grasses ancestral to wheat are known—dinkel and wild emmer. Both grow wild in mountainous countries, the former in the Balkans, the Crimea, Asia Minor, and the Caucasus, emmer further south in Palestine and perhaps in Persia.

The present distribution may, of course, be deceptive; climate has changed greatly since the time when cultivation began, and plant geography is dependent upon climate. Indeed, Vavilov, arguing from different premises, has proposed Afghanistan and Northwestern China as the original centers of wheat-growing. In any case, wild dinkel is the parent of a small, unsatisfying wheat, extensively cultivated in Central

Europe in prehistoric times and still grown in Asia Minor. A far superior grain may be got from the cultivation of emmer (*Triticum dicoccum*). Emmer seems to have been the oldest wheat cultivated in Egypt, in Asia Minor, and in Western Europe, and is often grown today. But the majority of the modern bread wheats belong to a third variety (*Triticum vulgare*), to which no wild ancestor is known. They may result from crosses between emmer and some unknown grass. The oldest wheat grains found in Mesopotamia, Turkestan, Persia, and India belong to this group.

The wild ancestors of barley are also mountain grasses. They have been reported from Marmarica in North Africa, Palestine, Asia Minor, Transcaucasia, Persia, Afghanistan, and Turkestan. Vavilov's methods would point to primary centers of barley cultivation in Abyssinia and Southeastern Asia. The questions where cultivation started and whether in one center or in several are still undecided. Because sickles have recently been found in cave dwellings in Palestine, accompanied by a set of tools appropriate to a food-gathering economy rather than to the culture normally associated with the first revolution, it is argued that cereal cultivation started in or near Palestine. But it is not impossible that these cave dwellers (termed Natufians) were just a backward tribe who had adopted some elements of culture from more progressive cultivators elsewhere, but had not yet thoroughly reorganized their economy.

As a revolution the introduction of a food-producing economy should affect the lives of all concerned, so as to be reflected in the population curve. Of course, no "vital statistics" have been recorded to prove that the expected increase of population did occur. But it is easy to see that it should. The community of food-gatherers had been restricted in size by the food supplies available—the actual number of game animals, fish, edible roots, and berries growing in its territory. No human effort could augment these supplies, whatever magicians might say. Indeed, improvements in the technique or intensification of hunting and collecting beyond a certain point would result in the progressive extermination of the game and an absolute diminution of supplies. And, in practice, hunting populations appear to be nicely adjusted to the resources at their disposal. Culivation at once breaks down the limits thus imposed. To increase the food supply it is only necessary to sow more seed, to bring more land under tillage. If there are more mouths to feed, there will also be more hands to till the fields.

Again, children become economically useful. To hunters

children are liable to be a burden. They have to be nourished for years before they can begin to contribute to the family larder effectively. But quite young toddlers can help in weeding fields and scaring off birds or trespassing beasts. If there are sheep and cattle, boys and girls can mind them. *A priori,* then, the probability that the new economy was accompanied

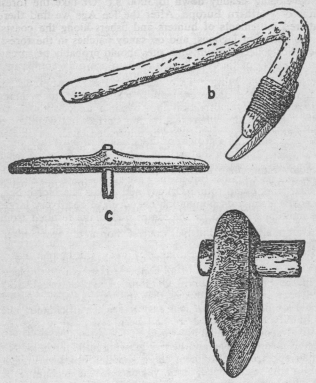

FIG. 4.—NEOLITHIC HOES. **a**

by an increase of population is very high. That population did really expand quite fast seems to be established by archaeology. Only so can we explain the apparent suddenness with which peasant communities sprang up in regions previously deserted or tenanted only by very sparse groups of collectors.

Round the lake that once filled the Fayum depression the number of Old Stone Age tools is certainly imposing. But they have to be spread over so many thousand years that the population they attest may be exiguous. Then quite abruptly the shore of a somewhat shrunken lake is found to be fringed with a chain of populous hamlets, all seemingly contemporary and devoted to farming. The Nile valley from the First Cataract down to Cairo is quickly lined with a chain of flourishing peasant villages, all seeming to start about the same time and all developing steadily down to 3000 B.C. Or take the forest plains of Northern Europe. After the Ice Age we find there scattered settlements of hunters and fishers along the coasts, on the shores of lagoons, and on sandy patches in the forest. The relics collected from such sites should probably be spread over a couple of thousand years, and so are only compatible with a tiny population. But then, within the space of a few centuries, Denmark first, and thereafter Southern Sweden, North Germany, and Holland, become dotted with tombs built of gigantic stones. It must have taken a considerable force to build such burial-places, and in fact some contain as many as 200 skeletons. The growth of the population must then have been rapid. It is true that in this case the first farmers, who were also the architects of the big stone graves, are supposed to have been immigrants. But as they are supposed to have come by boat from Spain round Orkney and across the North Sea, the actual immigrant population cannot have been very large. The multitude implied by the tombs must have resulted from the fecundity of a few immigrant families and that of the older hunters who had joined with these in exploiting the agricultural resources of the virgin north. Finally, the human skeletons assigned to the New Stone Age in Europe alone are several hundred times more numerous than those from the whole of the Old Stone Age. Yet the New Stone Age in Europe lasted at the outside 2000 years—less than one hundredth of the time assigned to the Old!

It would be tedious to pile up evidence; its implications are clear. It was only after the first revolution—but immediately thereafter—that our species really began to multiply at all fast. Certain other implications and consequences of this first or "neolithic" revolution can be considered later. It is desirable at this point to enter a caveat.

The adoption of cultivation must not be confused with the adoption of a sedentary life. It has been customary to contrast the settled life of the cultivator with the nomadic existence of the "homeless hunter." The contrast is quite fictitious. Last century the hunting and fishing tribes of the Pacific coasts of Canada possessed permanent villages of substantial, ornate, and almost luxurious wooden houses. The Magdalenians of France during the Ice Age certainly occupied the same cave over several generations. On the other hand, certain methods of cultivation impose a sort of nomadism upon their practitioners. To many peasants in Asia, Africa, and South America, even today, cultivation means simply clearing a patch of scrub or jungle, digging it up with a hoe or just a stick, sowing it, and then reaping the crop. The plot is not fallowed, still less manured, but just re-sown next year. Of course, under such conditions the yield declines conspicuously after a couple of seasons. Thereupon another plot is cleared, and the process repeated till that too is exhausted. Quite soon all the available land close to the settlement has been cropped to exhaustion. When that has happened, the people move away and start afresh elsewhere. Their household goods are simple enough to be easily transported. The houses themselves are flimsy hovels, probably grown foul by prolonged occupation, and can readily be replaced.

What has just been described is the most primitive form of cultivation, often termed hoe-culture or garden-culture. Nature soon posed a question to the first cultivators—the problem of soil exhaustion. The easiest way of dealing with the issue was to dodge it and move away. Actually that solution is perfectly satisfactory so long as there is plenty of cultivable land and the cultivator is content to do without such luxuries and refinements as impede migration. It was, of course, a nuisance to have to clear a new bit of forest every few years, but that was surely less trouble than thinking out a new solution. In any case this sort of cultivation prevailed throughout Europe north of the Alps in prehistoric times. It may have survived among some German tribes down to the beginning of our era; for the geographer Strabo remarks upon their readiness to shift their settlements. It is still practiced today, for example, among the rice-growing Nagas in Assam, among the Boro in the Amazon basin, and even by grain growers in the Sudan. Yet it is a wasteful method, and ultimately limits the population, since suitable land is nowhere unrestricted.

If nomadic garden-culture is the most primitive type of cultivation, it is not quite the simplest nor certainly the oldest. Throughout the great belt of countries now arid or desert, between the temperate forests of the north and the jungles of the tropics, the most suitable land for cultivation is often found on the alluvial soils deposited where intermittent torrents flow out from the hills on to the plains, and in the valleys of rivers that periodically overflow their banks. In that arid zone the muddy flood plains beside the great rivers and the silts, spreading out like a fan at the mouth of a torrent's gorge, form a welcome contrast to the unfertile sands or sterile rocks of the desert.

And on them the waters remaining from the floods take the place of the uncertain rains in providing the moisture needed for the germination and ripening of crops. And so in the Eastern Sudan the Hadendoa scattered millet seeds on the wet mud left by the Nile flood every autumn and just waited for the crop to sprout. Whenever a thunderstorm on Mount Sinai has brought down the Wady el Arish in flood, the desert Arabs hasten to sow barley grains in the freshly deposited silt and gathered a welcome crop.

Now under such conditions the floods, thus utilized, not only water the crop, they create fresh soil. The flood waters are yellow and muddy from the sediments which they have collected in their impetuous passage through the hills. As they spread out and flow more gently, the suspended mud is deposited as a deep silt on the inundated lands. The silt contains the chemical constituents that last year's crop had taken from the soil, which is thus renewed and refertilized. Under conditions of natural irrigation, the cultivator need not be nomadic. He can go on cultivating the same patches year after year provided they are flooded between each harvest.

Now the method of cultivation just described is possible precisely in the regions where wild ancestors of wheat and barley are probably native. Perry has cogently argued that irrigation is the oldest method of grain-growing. In particular, conditions in the Nile Valley would have been exceptionally favorable to the deliberate cultivation of cereals. The Nile, swollen by the monsoon rains on the Abyssinian plateau, overflows its banks with remarkable regularity every autumn. The flood arrives at a convenient season when the heat is no longer so intense as to scorch up young shoots. And so, Perry suggests, the reliable and timely Nile flood first prompted men to plant seeds deliberately and let them grow. Food-gatherers must have utilized grains of wild wheat and barley for food long before they started cultivating them. Handfuls of such seeds, scattered on the wet silt of the Nile's flood, would be the direct ancestors of all cultivated cereals. And natural irrigation would be the prototype of all systems of cultivation.

Perry's plausible and consistent account of the Egyptian origin of agriculture is, of course, just a theory supported by even less direct evidence than the Palestinian origin mentioned on p. 61. At the time of the oldest agricultural settlements in the Nile Valley and the rainfall in Hither Asia and North Africa was more generous than today, so that irrigation was by no means the sole method of getting crops to grow. The idea of cultivating cereals undoubtedly spread very rapidly; North Syria, Iraq, and the Persian plateau are studded with the ruins of agricul-

tural villages going back nearly, if not quite, as far as the oldest
of such villages in Egypt. Migratory garden-culture would explain this rapid diffusion quite simply. It is not so easy to see
how a system, developed under the exceptional conditions of
the Nile Valley, should have been transplanted to Persia and
Mesopotamia, with their very different and less favorable
circumstances. As to Europe, it is highly probable that the idea
of cultivation and the cereals cultivated were first introduced
by hoe-cultivators spreading from North Africa over Western
Europe and by others expanding from the Danube basin into
Belgium and Germany; for the wild ancestors of wheat and
barley are not to be expected north of the Balkans.

On the other hand, cultivation in Egypt was not so simple. In
its natural state the Nile Valley must have been a chain of
swamps, choked with reedy jungle that sheltered hippopotami
and other troublesome beasts. To make it cultivable the
swamps must be drained and cleared and their dangerous denizens driven out. Such an undertaking was possible to a well-
organized community of some size and equipped with efficient
tools. On the whole it looks as if cultivation dependent on the
Nile flood would be later than simple hoe-cultivation and derived therefrom. It is really unprofitable to speculate how,
where, and when the cultivation of cereals began. It is perhaps
slightly less futile to inquire how the primary form of food-
production was completed and transformed into mixed farming, assuming the theory enunciated on p. 59.

In practically all the oldest food-producing settlements examined by archaeologists in Europe, Hither Asia, and North
Africa, the basic industry is mixed farming; in addition to the
cultivation of cereals, animals are bred for food. This economy
is characteristic of the "neolithic" stage wherever such exist.
The food animals kept were not very varied: horned cattle,
sheep, goats, and swine. Comparatively few species—fowls are
the most important—have been added to the farmyards in subsequent periods or other countries. Horned cattle require
rather rich grass, but can live on well-watered steppes, in
natural irrigated valleys, and even in forests that are not too
dense. Pigs like swamps or woodlands; sheep and goats can
thrive under dry, though not absolutely desert, conditions, and
both are at home in hilly and mountainous country. Wild
goats probably once ranged all along the mountains that divide
Eurasia lengthwise, perhaps from the Pyrenees, or at least
from the Balkans eastwards to the Himalaya. Wild sheep lived
along the same chains, but in three distinct varieties. The
mouflon survivors in the Mediterranean islands and the hill
country of Hither Asia from Turkey to Western Persia; east

of the mouflon, in Turkestan, Afghanistan, and the Punjab, is the home of the urial; still farther east, in the mountains of Central Asia, lives the argal. In Africa no wild sheep is known. The oldest Egyptian sheep belong to the urial stock, as do the oldest European flocks; but the mouflon is represented side by side with the urial on early monuments from Mesopotamia. The reader will note that ancestors of our farmyard animals lived wild in most of the regions that seem likely to have comprised the cradle of grain-growing. But the absence of wild sheep from Africa makes Egypt unlikely as a starting point of mixing farming.

As already remarked, the period when the food-producing economy became established was one of climatic crises adversely affecting precisely that zone of arid sub-tropical countries where the earliest farmers appear, and where the wild ancestors of cultivated cereals and domestic animals actually lived. The melting of the European ice sheets and the contraction of the high pressures or anticyclones over them involved a northward shift in the normal path of the rain-bearing depressions from the Atlantic. The showers that had watered North Africa and Arabia were deflected over Europe. Desiccation set in. Of course the process was not sudden or catastrophic. At first and for long, the sole harbinger would be the greater severity and longer duration of periodical droughts. But quite a small reduction in the rainfall would work a devastating change in countries that were always relatively dry. It would mean the difference between continuous grasslands and sandy deserts interrupted by occasional oases.

A number of animals that could live comfortably with a twelve-inch annual rainfall would become a surplus population if the precipitation diminished by a couple of inches for two or three years on end. To get food and water, the grasseaters would have to congregate round a diminishing number of springs and streams—in oases. There they would be more exposed than ever to the attacks of beasts of prey—lions, leopards, and wolves—that would also gravitate to the oases for water. And they would be brought up against man too; for the same causes would force even hunters to frequent the springs and valleys. The huntsman and his prey thus find themselves united in an effort to circumvent the dreadful power of drought. But if the hunter is also a cultivator, he will have something to offer the famished beasts: the stubble of his freshly reaped fields will afford the best grazing in the oasis. Once the grains are garnered, the cultivator can tolerate half-starved mouflons or wild oxen trespassing upon his garden plots. Such will be too weak to run away, too thin to be worth killing for food. Instead, man can study their habits, drive off the lions and wolves that would prey upon them, and perhaps even offer them some surplus grain from his stores. The beasts, for their part, will grow tame and accustomed to man's proximity.

Hunters today, and doubtless in prehistoric times, have been accustomed to make pets of young wild animals for ritual ends or just for fun. Man has allowed the dog to frequent his camp in return for the offal of his prey and refuse from his feasts. Under the conditions of incipient desiccation the cultivator has the chance of attaching to his ménage not only isolated young beasts, but the remnants of complete flocks or herds, comprising animals of both sexes and all ages. If he just realizes the advantage of having a group of such half-tamed beasts hanging round the fringes of his settlement as a reserve of game easily caught, he will be on the way to domestication.

Next he must exercise restraint and discrimination in using this reserve of meat. He must refrain from frightening the beasts unnecessarily or killing the youngest and tamest. Once he begins to kill only the shyest and least amenable bulls or rams, he will have started selective breeding, eliminating untractable brutes, and consequently favoring the more docile. But he must also use his new opportunities of studying the life of the beasts at close range. He will thus learn about the processes of reproduction, the animals' needs of food and water. He must act upon his knowledge. Instead of merely driving the herd away when the time comes round for sowing his plots again, he must follow the beasts, guide them to suitable pastures and water, and continue to ward off predatory carnivora. It can thus be imagined how with lapse of time a flock or a herd should have been bred that was not only tame, but actually dependent upon man.

That result could happen only provided the peculiar climatic conditions continued long enough, and suitable animals were haunting human settlements. No doubt experiments were tried with various species; herds of antelopes and gazelles were kept by the Egyptians about 3000 B.C. These and other unknown experiments were fruitless. Luckly, cattle, sheep, goats, and pigs were included in the wild fauna of the desiccated regions in Asia. These did become firmly attached to man and ready to follow him.

At first the tame or domesticated beast would presumably be regarded only as a potential source of meat, an easily accessible sort of game. Other uses would be discovered later. It might be noticed that crops flourished best on plots that had been grazed over. Ultimately the value of dung as a fertilizer would

be realized. The process of milking can only have been discovered when men had had ample opportunity of studying
at close quarters the suckling of calves and lambs and kids.
But once the trick was grasped, milk would become a second
staple. It could be obtained without killing the beast, without
touching your capital. Selection would again be applied. The
best milkers would be spared, and their young reared in
preference to other calves, lambs, or kids. Still later the hair
of sheep or goats would win appreciation. It could be treated
by processes, perhaps originally applied to plant fibers, and
woven into cloth or else beaten into felt. Wool is entirely the
artificial product of selective breeding. On wild sheep it is
merely a down between the hairs. It was still unknown to the
Egyptians even after 3000 B.C. But in Mesopotamia sheep
were being bred for their wool before that date. The harnessing
of animals to bear burdens or draw plows and vehicles is a late
adaptation, and will be considered among the steps leading up
to the second revolution in human economy (p. 99).

The minimal characteristics of simple cultivation have already been considered. But these must now be pictured as combined with stock-breeding if we are to understand the basic
economy revealed in neolithic settlements in North Africa,
Hither Asia, and Europe. If the number of animals kept remains quite small, the account already given will hold good:
the animals will be put to graze on the stubble after the harvest
and at other seasons on natural pastures round the settlement.
Beyond telling off a few youths to look after the herd, the communal economy can be left as already described. But as soon
as the flocks exceed a low limit, special provision may have to
be made for them. Trees and scrub may be burned off to make
room for grass. In a river valley it may be thought worth-while
to clear or irrigate special meadows to serve as pasture for
cattle. Crops may be deliberately grown, harvested, and conserved to serve exclusively as fodder. Or the animals may be
driven far afield to find pastures in the dry season. In Mediterranean lands, Persia, and Asia Minor there is good summer
grazing on the hills which in winter are snow-clad. And so
sheep and cattle are driven up to hill pastures in the spring.
And now a regular company of the village's inhabitants must
accompany the herds to ward off wild beasts, to milk the cows
and ewes. The herders must generally take with them supplies
of grain and other equipment. In some cases the fraction of the
community that migrate with their gear to the summer pastures
is quite small. But in hot and dry countries, like Persia, parts
of the Eastern Sudan, and in the northwestern Himalayas, the
bulk of the community abandons its village in the stifling

valley and accompanies the herds to the cooler hills. Only a few stay behind to look after the fields and dwellings.

From this it is no far cry to a purely pastoral economy in which cultivation plays a negligible role. Pure pastoral nomadism is familiar, and is illustrated by several peoples in the Old World; the Bedouin of Arabia and Mongolian tribes of Central Asia are the best-known examples. How old such a mode of life may be is uncertain. Pastoralists are not likely to leave many vestiges by which the archaeologist could recognize their presence. They tend to use vessels of leather and basketry instead of pots, to live in tents instead of in excavated shelters or huts supported by stout timber posts or walls of stone or brick. Leather vessels and baskets have as a rule no chance of surviving; tents need not even leave deep post holes to mark where they once stood. (Though wood decays, modern archaeology can recognize the hole made by a post five thousand years ago.)

The failure to recognize prehistoric settlement sites or groups of relics belonging to pure pastoralists is not in itself any proof that such did not exist. To that extent the postulate of the "historical school," that pure pastoralism and pure hoe-culture were originally practiced independently by separate peoples and that mixed farming resulted from their subsequent fusion, is irrefutable. Yet Forde has recently emphasized the instability of pure pastoralism. Many typical pastoral tribes today, like the patriarchs in Genesis, actually cultivate grain, though in an incidental and rather casual manner. If they grow no grain themselves, pastoral nomads are almost always economically dependent upon settled peasant villages. The cultivators may be tributaries or serfs to the pastoralists, but they are essential to their subsistence.

Whatever its origin, stock-breeding gave man control over his own food supply in the same way was cultivation did. In mixed farming it becomes an equal partner in the food-producing economy. But just as the term "cultivation" covers many distinct modes of gaining a livelihood, so the single phrase "mixed farming" marks an equal disparity and diversity. The several different modes of cultivation may be combined in varying degrees with distinct attitudes to the livestock. The diversity of the permutations and combinations has just been suggested. The multiplicity of concrete applications of the food-producing economy must never be forgotten.

It must be remembered, too, that food-production does not at once supersede food-gathering. If today hunting is only a ritual sport and game is a luxury for the rich, fishing is still a great industry, contributing directly to everybody's diet. At first hunting, fowling, fishing, the collection of fruits, snails, and grubs continued to be essential activities in the food-quest of any food-producing group. Grain and milk began as mere supplements to a diet of game, fish, berries, nuts, and ants' eggs. Probably at first cultivation was an incidental activity of the women while their lords were engaged in the really serious business of the chase. Only slowly did it win the status of an independent and ultimately predominant industry. When the archaeological record first reveals neolithic communities in Egypt and Iran, survivals from the food-gathering régime clearly stand on an equal footing with grain-growing and stock-breeding. Only subsequently does their economic importance decline. After the second revolution, hunting and fowling have become, as with us, ritual sports, or else, like fishing, specialized industries practiced by groups within the community or by independent societies, economically dependent upon an agricultural civilization.

Two other aspects of the simple food-producing economy deserve attention. In the first place, food-production, even in its simplest form, provides an opportunity and a motive for the accumulation of a surplus. A crop must not be consumed as soon as it is reaped. The grains must be conserved and eked out so as to last till the next harvest, for a whole year. And a proportion of every crop must be set aside for seed. The conservation is easy. But it means on the one hand forethought and thrift, on the other receptacles for storage. These are quite as essential as, and may actually be more elaborate than, dwellings. In the neolithic villages of the Fayum, perhaps the oldest of their kind, excavated silos, lined with straw basketry or matting, are the most substantial constructions that have survived.

Again, livestock that has been laboriously carried over the dry season must not be indiscriminately slaughtered and devoured. The young cows and ewes at least must be spared and reared to provide milk and to augment the herd or flock. Once these ideas have been driven home, the production and accumulation of a surplus are much easier for food-producers than for food gatherers. The yield of crops and of herds soon outstrips the immediate needs of the community. The storage of grain, the conservation of live meat "on the hoof" is much simpler, especially in a warm climate, than the preservation of stocks of slaughtered game. The surplus thus gathered will help to tide the community over bad seasons; it will form a reserve against droughts and crop failures. It will serve to support a growing population. Ultimately it may constitute a basis for rudimentary trade, and so pave the way to a second revolution.

Secondly, the economy is entirely self-sufficing. The simple food-producing community is not dependent for any necessity of life on imports obtained by barter or exchange from another group. It produces and collects all the food it needs. It relies on raw materials available in its immediate vicinity for the simple equipment it demands. Its constituent members or households manufacture the requisite implements, utensils, and weapons.

This economic self-sufficiency does not necessarily spell isolation. The variations in the simple food-producing economy already indicated, the simultaneous pursuit of several methods of obtaining nourishment by different groups, are liable to bring the several communities concerned into mutual contact. Driving their flocks to summer pastures, the herdsmen from one village are likely to meet their counterparts from another. On hunting expeditions across the desert, huntsmen from one oasis may cross parties from another. In such ways the isolation of each community is liable to be broken down. Far from being a scattering of discrete units, the neolithic world should be viewed as a continuous chain of communities. Each would be linked to its neighbors on either side by recurrent, if infrequent and irregular, contacts.

The simple food-producing economy just described is an abstraction. Our picture is based on a selection of supposedly distinctive traits from materials afforded by ethnographers' observations on modern "savages" and inferences from particular archaeological sites. The precise stage of economic development here adumbrated may never have been fully realized in precisely this concrete form. Archaeology alone could justify the presentation of a "neolithic" economy as a universal historical stage in the progress towards modern civilization. But all archaeology can do at present is to isolate temporary phases in what was really a continuous process. We have tacitly assumed that similar phases were realized nearly simultaneously in several areas. But in prehistoric times such simultaneity cannot be proved, even in the cases of regions so close together as Tasa in Middle Egypt, the Fayum, and the Delta. Strict parallelism in time between Egypt and, say, North Syria would be hard to establish. To claim it as between Egypt and North Europe would be almost certainly false; our best examples of a simple food-producing economy in Britain or Belgium are to be dated in terms of solar years perhaps thirty centuries later than their counterparts in Egypt. And we have deliberately cited contemporary savage groups as illustrating the same economic stage.

Archaeology has disclosed communities whose basic economy approximates to that just described in the Nile Valley at Tasa, on the western edge of the Delta, and on the shore of an old lake in the Fayum, in the rain belt of North Syria between Aleppo and Mosul, and on the slopes of the Iranian plateau perhaps 7000 years ago. Rather later we find the same economy established in Crete, on the plateau of Asia Minor, and in Thessaly and other parts of Mainland Greece. Still later it becomes traceable in Spain, on the Black Earth belt of the Ukraine and Bessarabia, around the Lower Danube valley, in the Hungarian plain, and then throughout Central Europe wherever patches of so-called löss offered fertile soils not too heavily wooded. The same economy spread widely over Western Europe from Spain to Southern England and Belgium. It emerges later still in Denmark, North Germany, and Sweden —perhaps not before 2000 B.C. Similar communities, recently identified in Western China, need not be much older. The Maoris of New Zealand were still on this economic plane when Captain Cook landed near the end of the eighteenth century A.D.!

All the groups of simple food-producers recognized by archaeology are distinguished from one another by very marked differences. Archaeologists divide them into a bewildering variety of "cultures." Each has its own distinctive types of tools, vessels, weapons, and ornaments, its own peculiar art and burial rites. Even the applications of the basic economy differ from group to group. Nomadic garden-culture was, for instance, the rule in Western Europe, on the löss lands of Central Europe, in the Ukraine, and in Western China—all temperate regions. In Crete or Thessaly even the oldest settlements seem relatively permanent. Again, in Western Europe the breeding of cattle, sheep, and swine, and hunting were at least on an equal footing with grain-growing. On the Central European löss domestic animals seem to have played at first a minor role in the food supply, and game an altogether negligible one. The neolithic Chinese kept only pigs.

Among the neolithic Egyptians at Tasa cattle and sheep bones were found in plenty, but no remains of pig. That animal was, however, plentiful in the contemporary settlements in the Fayum and on the Delta's edge. Again, the grains grown differ—emmer wheat in Egypt, Assyria, Western and Northern Europe, dinkel in the Danube basin, bread-wheat perhaps in Syria and Turkestan. Thus there is no such thing as a neolithic civilization. Various human groups of different racial composition, living under diverse conditions of climate and soil, have adopted the same ground ideas and adapted them differently to their several environments.

The differences which so clearly separate neolithic cultures are not surprising in view of the distinctive character of the economy, the self-sufficiency of each community. Because each group was economically independent of any neighbors, it could remain isolated from them. And in such isolation each group could work out its own arts and crafts, its own styles and institutions independent of the rest. Only the most bigoted evolutionist will contend that these independent developments would converge everywhere to like results. The reverse may be actually observed. If one studies in detail several closely allied neolithic groups—on the Central European löss, for example—one notices a continual divergence, the multiplication of individualized groups each differing from one another ever more pronouncedly in the fashionable shape for vases, the style of their decoration, and so on.

Nevertheless, the possible isolation was never actually realized—perhaps, indeed, complete economic self-sufficiency was nowhere attained. Everywhere intercourse between adjacent groups is attested to the archaeologist by an interchange of objects. Such might result from accidental contacts between herdsmen and hunters, such as we have anticipated, from formal visits, from the practice of seeking a wife outside one's own village (exogamy), and so on. It might lead up to a sort of irregular trade through which objects might travel great distances. So the neolithic settlements on the Fayum lake shells were brought both from the Mediterranean and the Red Sea. Bracelets made from the shell of a Mediterranean mussel, *Spondylus gaederopi,* have been found in neolithic graves even in Bohemia and South Germany.

The point is that such trade was not an integral part of the community's economic life; the articles it brought were in some sense luxuries, non-essentials. Yet the intercourse thus attested was of vital importance to human progress; it provided channels whereby ideas from one society might reach another, whereby foreign materials might be compared, whereby, in fact, culture itself might be diffused. Indeed, "neolithic civilization" in part owes its expansion to the prior existence amongst still sparser hunting communities of a rudimentary web of intercourse.

In exceptional cases communication between separate groups of the kind here envisaged might lead to more regular "trade" and to intercommunal specialization even within the framework of the neolithic economy. In England, Belgium, and France archaeologists have discovered neolithic flint mines. The miners probably cultivated plants and bred cattle in the intervals of mining. But it is quite certain that they were not producing for themselves alone, but exporting their flints to a wider market. Nevertheless, where seas, forests, or wooded mountains intervened, intercourse in neolithic times must generally have been very infrequent and the percolation of ideas exceedingly slow. Only in the arid zone round the Mediterranean and east thereof was intercourse at all rapid or extensive.

Thus "neolithic times" may mean anything between 6000 B.C and A.D. 1800. "Neolithic civilization" is a dangerous term applicable to a huge variety of cultural groups, all more or less on the same economic plane. Still, at sites like Tasa, the Fayum lake, and the lowest levels at Arpachiyah in Assyria the economy just outlined does seem actually to represent the highest form of organization attained anywhere at that precise moment. Elsewhere and later we still find communities exhibiting the same fundamental economic structure. And all have more than mere abstractions of economics in common. It is true that the other agreements are only slightly less abstract. Still, it is worth-while ignoring the differences of their concrete applications and considering some of these general traits common to many "neolithic" societies. The outstanding common features are wood-working, pottery manufacture, and a textile industry.

At the time when the neolithic revolution makes itself manifest, when cultivation first becomes perceptible, North Africa and Hither Asia were still enjoying a higher rainfall than today; trees still grew in regions now treeless. At the same time, in Europe, forests had replaced the tundras and steppes of the Ice Age. Man was obliged to deal with timber. The response to this stimulus was the creation of the "polished stone celt" (axe or adze), which to the older archaeologists was the distinctive mark of "neolithic times." The implement is a large slice or pebble of fine-grained stone, one end of which has been ground down to form a sharp cutting edge. It was hafted into the end of a stick or an antler to form an axe or an adze.

In the later part of the Old Stone Age axe-like tools seem to have been unknown. The ground stone celt does not seem to derive directly from the "hand axe" of flaked stone or flint current earlier in the Old Stone Age. The essence of the neolithic tool is that its edge is sharpened by grinding. The new technique might be suggested by effects observed on stone rubbers used for grinding grains on other stones. Or perhaps for digging up the garden plots a split pebble was lashed on to the end of a stick to make a sort of hoe; then the end of the pebble might be rubbed sharp by friction with sandy soil. But, though neolithic celts are almost invariably found in the oldest settlements of simple food-producers, it is not certain that the implement is really a result of the new economy. Axe-like tools are found, for instance, on the Baltic, long before there are any indications of farming. The models there seem to be provided by implements of bone and antler, also sharpened by polishing. Ground stone axes and adzes were certainly used by some denizens of the North European forest who still bred no animals for food and cultivated no plants. And outside Europe many typical food-gatherers, including even the aborigines of Australia, used ground stones axes. On the other hand, the Natufians of Palestine, who certainly reaped something, presumably a cereal, with sickles, possessed no axes. The ground stone celt is not therefore an infallible sign of the neolithic economy in the sense here used of self-sufficing food production.

Still, wherever it arose, the ground stone celt provided a tough implement and a resistant edge that would not be chipped or blunted by a few blows. It enabled man to hew and to shape timber. Carpentry could begin. Plows, wheels, plank-boats, wooden houses all require axes and adzes for their manufacture. The invention of the ground stone celt was an essential pre-condition for these later achievements.

The preparation and storage of cereal foods may be supposed to have put a premium upon vessels which would at once stand heat and hold liquids. A universal feature of neolithic communities seems to have been the manufacture of pots. (Such were not, however, used by the Natufians of Palestine.) Pottery may, indeed, have been discovered before the rise of the food-producing economy. It might have originated in the accidental burning of a basket plastered with clay to make it water-tight. A couple of small fragments allegedly found in an Old Stone Age layer in Kenya suggest this possibility. But it is only in neolithic times that pot-making is attested on a large scale; a neolithic site is generally strewn with fragments of broken pottery.

The new industry has great significance for human thought and for the beginning of science. Pot-making is perhaps the earliest conscious utilization by man of a chemical change. The essence of the process is the expulsion by heat of some molecules of water (termed the "water of constitution") from the hydrated silicate of aluminum which is the chemist's name for potter's clay. A lump of clay when wet is completely plastic; it will disintegrate in excess of water and crumble to powder if dried. When the "water of constitution," chemically combined in it, is expelled rather above 600° C. the material loses its plasticity altogether; the whole lump solidifies, and will keep its shape wet or dry unless deliberately and laboriously broken up by crushing or pounding. The essence of the potter's craft is that she can mold a piece of clay into any shape she desires and then give that shape permanence by "firing" (*i.e.* heating to over 600° C.).

To early man this change in the quality of the material must have seemed a sort of magic transubstantiation—the conversion of mud or dust into stone. It may have prompted some philosophical questions as to the meaning of substance and sameness. How is the plastic clay the same substance as the hard but brittle earthenware? The pot you put into the fire has much the same shape as what you draw out, but the color has changed and the texture is quite different.

The discovery of pottery consisted essentially in finding out how to control and utilize the chemical change just mentioned. But, like all other discoveries, its practical application involves others. To be able to mold your clay you must wet it; but if you put your damp plastic pot straight into the fire, it will crack. The water, added to the clay to make it plastic, must be dried out gently in the sun or near the fire, before the vessel can be baked. Again, the clay has to be selected and prepared. If it contains too large grits, it will not model easily nor yield a handsome or serviceable pot; some process of washing must be devised to eliminate coarse material. On the other hand, if the clay contains no grit, it will stick to the fingers in molding and crack in firing. To avoid this danger some gritty material —sand, powdered stone or shell, chopped straw, what is termed a "temper"—must be added.

In the process of firing, the clay changes not only its physical consistency, but also its color. The latter change is determined partly by chemical impurities in the material, partly by the process of firing. Most clays contain some iron oxide. If the air has free access to the pot while it is hot, the vessel will come out with a reddish hue because the iron will be oxidized to form the red ferric oxide. But if the pot be surrounded during firing with glowing charcoal and the gases given off during imperfect combustion, the iron salts will be reduced, and the product will be gray, because ferroso-ferric oxide is black. A dark color may also be produced by free carbon in the clay. That may be derived from the charring of vegetable or organic impurities in the raw material, or from soot from the fire soaking into the pores of the red-hot earthenware, or from fats or dung deliberately applied to the vase surface while it is still hot. Man had to learn to control such changes as these and to utilize them to enhance the beauty of the vessel.

At first, local conditions, the sort of clay and fuel available on the spot, would be allowed to determine the color of the pot. Average clays, burned in the smoky brushwood fires of well-watered regions, yield black or dirty gray vessels. Under rather drier climates reds and brown can be produced. The hot fires made from thorny Mediterranean or desert plants easily yield pale buff, pinkish, or greenish wares. Subsequently the potter learns how to produce such effects at will or to enhance them for the embellishment of the vessel. She might, for instance, cover the vase's surface with a thin layer—a "slip" or wash—of selected clay, rich in iron oxides, in order to produce a good red ware. She might even apply such specially prepared clays with a brush so as to outline painted patterns. It must be remembered that the effect of color painted on an unfired vessel is quite different from that of the final product. Vase-painting is no simple art; the artist has to forecast in advance what the fired pot is going to look like. The feat was early achieved in Hither Asia. It was a long time before painted pottery could be manufactured in temperate regions where the natural fuel gave a smoky flame.

There the light ground needed to show up painted decoration could only be achieved with the aid of a further invention —a built oven or kiln in which the vases can be raised to 900° or 1000° C., and yet kept out of contact with the flames. Such a device is not attested for the earliest neolithic communities; it does not reach Central or Western Europe till the Iron Age.

Thus the potter's craft, even in its crudest and most generalized form, was already complex. It involved an appreciation of a number of distinct processes, the application of a whole constellation of discoveries. Only a few of these have been even mentioned. At the risk of boring the reader, we must note one more. The shaping of the pot itself is not so easy as it sounds. Quite small vessels can, of course, be kneaded and molded, mud-pie fashion, out of a lump of clay. Or a coating of clay can be spread over an open basket or a half-gourd; when it has dried, the form can be removed, and you have an open dish or platter ready for firing.

But if anything larger is desired, or a vessel with a narrow neck like a bottle or jug, such elementary processes no longer suffice: the vessel must be built up. In neolithic Europe and Asia this was generally done by the ring method; after the base had been molded, rings of clay of the desired diameter were prepared. One was attached to the base and then another set on the top edge of this, and so on. It is a slow process. The rings must be fairly wet and plastic when they are put on. But as soon as one ring is in place, you must pause and let it dry and harden—but not too much—before adding the next story.

The mere construction of a large pot may take several days.

The constructive character of the potter's craft reacted on human thought. Building up a pot was a supreme instance of creation by man. The lump of clay was perfectly plastic; man could mold it as he would. In making a tool of stone or bone he was always limited by the shape and size of the original material; he could only take bits away from it. No such limitations restrict the activity of the potter. She can form her lump as she wishes; she can go on adding to it without any doubts as to the solidity of the joins. In thinking of "creation," the free activity of the potter in "making form where there was no form" constantly recurs to man's mind; the similes in the Bible taken from the potter's craft illustrate the point.

In practice the potter's freedom to create was not at first fully utilized. Fancy cannot work in a vacuum. What it creates must be like something already known. Moreover, pots were generally made by women and for women, and women are particularly suspicious of radical innovations. So the earliest pots are obvious imitations of familiar vessels made from other materials—from gourds, from bladders, membranes, and skins, from basketry and wickerwork, or even from human skulls. To enhance the resemblance, the grass sling in which a gourd, like a modern Chianti flask, was carried, the stitching of the "wine-skin," or the interlacing fibres of the basket were often imitated by patterns incised or painted on the pot. Thus the vessel in the fresh material came to look less new-fangled and outlandish to the prudent housewife!

Among the remains of the earliest neolithic villages of Egypt and Hither Asia we find the first indications of a textile industry. Manufactured garments, woven out of linen, or later wool, begin to compete with dressed skins or skirts of leaves as protection against cold and sun. For this to be possible another complex of discoveries and inventions is requisite, a further body of scientific knowledge must be practically applied. In the first place, a suitable material was needed, a fibrous substance that would yield long threads. The neolithic villagers on the Fayum lake were already using flax. They must have selected this from all other plants and begun to cultivate it deliberately in addition to growing cereals. Another variety of flax may have been discovered and grown in Asia. A local European flax was cultivated and utilized in Switzerland in neolithic times.

Other materials must have been tried. Cotton was certainly being grown in the Indus valley soon after 3000 B.C. Wool, as already noted, was used in Mesopotamia about the same time. Before wool-bearing sheep had been produced by selective

breeding, the hairs of sheep and goats may have served for the
production of a sort of cloth, since hair can be woven. A textile
industry thus not only requires the knowledge of special substances like flax, cotton, and wool, but also the breeding of
special animals and the cultivation of particular plants.

Among the prerequisite inventions a device for spinning is
important. The little discs of stone or pottery, termed whorls,
that served to weight the end of a spindle, like miniature fly-
wheels, generally constitute the sole tangible proof of the existence of a textile industry that an archaeologist can hope to
find. Only very exceptional conditions can preserve actual
textile products or the wooden implements used in their production.

Of these the most essential is a loom. It is, indeed, possible
to produce a sort of cloth with the aid of a frame by a sort of
glorified plaiting process similar to that employed in making
mats. Blankets of dogs' hair were actually produced in this way
by food-gathering tribes on the northwest coast of Canada
last century. But in the Old World a true loom goes back to
neolithic times. Now a loom is quite an elaborate piece of
machinery—much too elaborate to be described here. Its use
is no less complicated. The invention of the loom was one of
the great triumphs of human ingenuity. Its inventors are name-
less, but they made an essential contribution to the capital
stock of human knowledge, an application of science that only
to the unthinking seems too trivial to deserve the name.

All the foregoing industries require for their exercise a
technical skill that can only be acquired by training and practice. Yet all were household crafts. In our hypothetical neolithic stage there would be no specialization of labor—at most
a division of work between the sexes. And that system can still
be seen at work today. Among hoe-cultivators the women generally till the fields, build up and fire the pots, spin, and weave;
men look after animals, hunt and fish, clear the plots for cultivation, and act as carpenters, preparing their own tools and
weapons. But, of course, to such a generalization there are
many exceptions: among the Yoruba, for instance, weaving is
in the hands of men.

All the industries named, from garden culture to weaving,
have been rendered possible only by the accumulation of experience and the application of deductions therefrom. Each
and all repose on practical science. Moreover, the exercise of
each craft is throughout regulated and directed by a constantly
expanding body of practical science. The appropriate lore is
handed on from parent to child for generation after generation.
The cultivator, for instance, must know in practice what soil

it is most profitable to till, when to break up the ground, how to distinguish young grain shoots from sprouting weeds, and a host of other details. The young potter must learn to find and choose proper clay, how to clean it, with what proportion of water and grit it should be mixed, and so on.

Thus there grows up to be handed on a great body of craft lore—snippets of botany, geology, and chemistry, one might say. If we may judge from the procedure of modern barbarians, the legitimate deductions from experience are inextricably mixed up with what we should call useless magic. Each operation of every craft must be accompanied by the proper spells and the prescribed ritual acts. All this body of rules, practical and magical, forms part of the craft tradition. It is handed on from parent to child by example and by precept. The daughter helps her mother at making pots, watches her closely, imitates her, and receives from her lips oral directions, warnings, and advice. The applied sciences of neolithic times were handed on by what today we should call a system of apprenticeship.

The neolithic crafts have been presented as household industries. Yet the craft traditions are not individual, but collective traditions. The experience and wisdom of all the community's members are constantly being pooled. In a modern African village the housewife does not retire into seclusion in order to build up and fire her pots. All the women of the village work together, chatting and comparing notes; they even help one another. The occupation is public; its rules are the result of communal experience. And so in prehistoric times all the pots from a given neolithic village exhibit a monotonous uniformity. They bear the stamp of a strong collective tradition rather than of individuality. [1]

And the neolithic economy as a whole cannot exist without co-operative effort. The heavier labor of clearing patches in a forest or draining a marsh must be a collective undertaking. The digging of drains, the defense of the settlement against wild beasts or floods, must again be communal responsibilities. The dwellings in neolithic villages both in Egypt and in Western Europe have been proved to be arranged in a regular order, not scattered about indiscriminately. All this implies some social organization to co-ordinate and control the communal activities. What that organization was we can never know exactly. One assertion seems plausible.

The effective unit of social organization in pure neolithic times was generally very small. A typical Thessalian village,

---

[1] Yet certain "neolithic" communities today recognize the proprietary rights of individuals or families to particular patterns, ceremonies, or processes.

rather advanced in the period, covered an area of 100 by 45 metres, or just over one acre! Several neolithic cemeteries have been fully explored in Central Europe. None contained more than twenty graves. (Of course, we do not know how long the settlement was occupied nor how many generations are represented in each cemetery.) Among modern representatives of garden-cultivation a tendency for the village to break up has been noted by ethnographers. Some of the young men hive off with their wives and start a new village of their own. They like the freedom of their new settlement, in which they are exempt from the authority and oversight of their elders. Then, founding a new village with plots of virgin jungle close to the dwellings saves long walks to the gardens, such as become necessary when the original village is populous and the nearest land has already been used up. On the whole the separation would be convenient—provided, of course, there was land available. In neolithic times there was as yet no shortage.

Undoubtedly the co-operative activities involved in "neolithic" life found outward expression in social and political institutions. Undoubtedly such institutions were consolidated and reinforced by magico-religious sanctions, by a more or less coherent system of beliefs and superstitions, by what Marxists would call an ideology. The new forces controlled by man as the result of the neolithic revolution and the knowledge gained and applied in the exercise of the new crafts must have reacted upon man's outlook. They must have modified his institutions and his religion. But precisely what form neolithic institutions and beliefs assumed is unknowable.

Deductions of what ought to be appropriate to the neolithic economy need not correspond to historical reality: the precise forms of the English constitution and of English protestantism in the nineteenth century cannot be deduced from the capitalist system. Generalizations from observations made on a few ancient sites can claim no universal validity. Inferences from institutions and rites, observed among barbarous tribes today, do not certainly, or even probably, give clues to the political and mental life of other barbarous tribes who, 6000 years earlier, had reached a similar stage of economic development. Institutions, beliefs, and theories notoriously tend to lag behind actual practice. There was, as has already been insisted, no "neolithic" civilization, only a multitude of different concrete applications of a few very general principles and notions.

If barbarous tribes today are still content to secure a livelihood by the same "neolithic" method as 6000 years ago, there is no guarantee that their political and religious life has been equally stagnant. On the contrary, subsequent revolutions have had worldwide effects, for reasons indicated on p. 136. Five thousand years give ample time for some results of the second revolution to percolate even to Australia. There is positive evidence that some of the material achievements due to the second revolution were adopted by peoples whose economic organization remained unaffected as a whole. All typical hoe-cultivators in Africa, for instance, have been using iron for centuries. The second revolution, we shall see, evoked vigorous systems of magico-religious beliefs. The spread of great stone graves among neolithic peoples in Western and Northern Europe is most plausibly explained by repercussions of the beliefs then formulated in the Ancient East. Some authorities would find traces of such beliefs even among food-gathering aborigines in Australia and America. To use contemporary barbarians' religions as evidence for the religion of Egypt or Hither Asia in 5000 B.C. would be possible only if the diffusion of ideas were entirely eliminated.

We shall not therefore attempt a description of "the neolithic polity" and "the neolithic religion." It is really unlikely that any such existed. The "neolithic revolution" was not a catastrophe, but a process. Its several stages were doubtless modifying the social institutions and magico-religious ideas of food-gatherers and hunters. But it would be long before any new system or systems, more appropriate to the nascent economy, became firmly established. Ere then the second revolution may already have been beginning. It was perhaps the very absence of rigid ideologies and deeply-rooted institutions that permitted the rapid progress from self-sufficing villages to industrial and commercial cities in less than 2000 years.

Firmly entrenched institutions, passionately held superstitions, are notoriously inimical to social change and the scientific advances that make it necessary. And the force of such reaction in a community seems to be inversely proportional to the community's economic security. A group always on the brink of starvation dare not risk change. The least deviation from the traditional procedures that have been found to yield the essential modicum of subsistence may imperil the whole group. It would be just as dangerous to antagonize the mysterious magic powers that control the weather by omitting a rite or a sacrifice as to omit poisoning the arrowhead that is to slay an elephant.

Now, even after the first revolution, life remained very precarious for the little group of self-sufficing peasants. A drought, a hailstorm, a blight might mean famine. Such peasants had no world market to draw upon, so that deficiencies of crops in one area could be compensated by a surplus in another. They had still only a limited variety of sources of food. All their several crops, their herds, and their game might easily be affected by the same catastrophe. The reserves in store were never large. A self-sufficing peasant community is inevitably fully conscious of its immediate dependence on the powers that bring rain and sunshine, thunder and hurricane. But these act capriciously and terribly. At all costs they must be compelled, cajoled, or conciliated.

Now, once you can make yourself believe that you have found a system of magic to achieve that compulsion, or a ritual to ensure that conciliation, the belief becomes a solace in the terrors of life that one dare not surrender. Had such magics and rituals been firmly established, they would surely have retarded the spread of the second revolution. After it, firmly rooted beliefs—for instance, in the efficacy of astrology and the potency of divine kings and ancestral spirits—did impede the growth of true science and the establishment of an inter-urban international economy. But perhaps the first revolution was still just sapping confidence in the necessity of hunters' magic and its political consequences when the disturbing ideas and discoveries heralding the second revolution were emerging. Perhaps any new system of organization and belief, adapted to the neolithic economy, had not become established and rooted when the economy itself began to dissolve in the Orient.

Nevertheless, certain hints are available as to institutions that did or did not subsist in neolithic times. Sometimes they seem to have reacted upon the form taken by the second revolution. That many institutions were taken over from the older order is only natural. In the Nile Valley there is indirect evidence of the survival of a system of totemic clans. The later neolithic villages seem to have been the settlements belonging to such clans. When in historical times the villages became the capitals of parishes (nomes), they bore names like Elephantine and Falcontown (Hierakonpolis), taken apparently from the totem of the localized clan, the elephant and the falcon. The standards of the parishes were clan emblems, and even in prehistoric times such emblems figure upon the vases. Such a clan system is not uncommon among simple food-producers today, and may be a genuine survival from neolithic times. But that all neolithic communities were organized as totemic clans cannot be asserted.

Of chieftainship there is no definite evidence in early neolithic cemeteries or villages. There are, that is to say, no outstandingly wealthy graves, evidently belonging to a person of rank, and no dwellings that could pass for palaces. The great stone graves of Western and Northern Europe which do look princely belong to a time when ideas proper to the second revolution were being diffused, and they are probably inspired thereby. Houses larger than the normal have been noted in some neolithic villages in Europe, but they may be communal lodges of clubs, like the bachelors' houses of the Pacific Islanders, rather than princely residences. Nor is there unambiguous evidence of warfare. Weapons are certainly often found in neolithic graves and settlements. But were they arms of war or merely implements of the chase? Woman's increasing share in the provision of food for the community may have raised also the social status of the sex. But that too is uncertain.

As to the magico-religious notions that held neolithic communities together, a few guesses may be hazarded. The tendance of the dead, going far back into the Old Stone Age, may have assumed a deeper significance in the new. In the case of several neolithic groups, indeed, no burials have been discovered. But generally the dead were carefully interred in built or excavated graves, either grouped in cemeteries near the settlement or dug close to the individual dwellings. The dead are normally provided with utensils or weapons, vases of food and drink, and toilet articles. In prehistoric Egypt pictures of animals and objects are painted on the funerary vases. They presumably had the same magic significance as the cave painting and rock-carvings of Old Stone Age hunters. In historical times they were transferred to the walls of the tomb, and then attached texts show that they were really designed to ensure to the dead the continued enjoyment of the services they depict.

Such tendance denotes an attitude to the ancestral spirits that goes back to far older periods. But now the earth in which the ancestors' remains lie buried is seen as the soil from which the community's food supply magically springs each year. The ancestral spirits must surely be regarded as assisting in the crops' germination.

Fertility cults, magic rites to assist or compel the forces of reproduction, may have become more prominent than ever in neolithic times. Small figurines of women, carved in stone or ivory, with the sexual characters well marked, have been noted in camps of the Old Stone Age. But similar figures, now generally modeled in clay, are very common in neolithic settlements and graves. They are often termed "mother goddesses." Was the earth from whose womb the young grain sprouts really conceived in the likeness of a woman with whose generative functions man is certainly familiar?

The early Oriental civilizations periodically celebrated with great pomp a "sacred marriage," the nuptial union of a "king" and a "queen," who on this occasion represented divinities. Their union not only symbolized, but also magically ensured and compelled, the fertilization of the earth, that she might bring forth her fruits in due season. But the seed must die and be buried before it can sprout and multiply. A human representative of the grain, a "corn king," was once slain and buried. His place was taken by a young successor who should stand for the growing crops till he too must lie like the seed in the ground. These magical rites, these dramatic representations of the death and rebirth of the grain, were often mitigated in practice by historical times. But they can be discerned behind many early myths, and in neolithic times may have been observed literally. Yet they might pave the way to political power. The "corn king" may claim by magic to have attained immortality. Then he is a secular king, too, entitled to the dignity of a god.

Finally, cultivation may have required a closer observation of the seasons, a more accurate division of time, the year. Agricultural operations are essentially seasonal, and their success is largely dependent upon the time of their performance. But the proper season is determined by the sun, not by the moon's phases, which provide a calendar for hunters. In northerly latitudes the changes in the sun's path between the solstices are conspicuous enough to provide clues as to the seasons. The observation of such clues would emphasize the sun's role as ruler of the seasons and guarantee his divinity.

But near the tropics the sun's movement is less striking. There the stars, always visible in those cloudless skies, provide a more obvious means of determining and dividing the solar year. You note that certain stars of constellations take up a significant position in the sky at the time when experience suggests you should plant your crops, others when you may expect rain to ripen them. By so using the stars as guides, men may have come to the belief that they actually influenced terrestrial affairs. You confuse connection in time with causal connection. Because the star Sirius is seen on the horizon at dawn when the Nile flood arrives, it is inferred that Sirius causes the Nile flood. Astrology is based on this sort of confusion. In Mesopotamia the sign for deity was a star. Cults of the sun and of the stars may have been growing up in this sort of way in neolithic times. But really we do not know to what extent man had yet formulated any idea of divinity. It is difficult to distinguish ideas elaborated and diffused after the second revolution from those developed by the first.

CHAPTER VI

PRELUDE TO THE SECOND REVOLUTION

THE neolithic revolution, just described, was the climax of a long process. It has to be presented as a single event because archaeology can only recognize the result; the several steps leading up thereto are beyond the range of direct observation. A second revolution transformed some tiny villages of self-sufficing farmers into populous cities, nourished by secondary industries and foreign trade, and regularly organized as States. Some of the episodes which ushered in this transformation can be discerned, if dimly, by prehistory. The scene of the drama lies in the belt of semi-arid countries between the Nile and the Ganges. Here epoch-making inventions seem to have followed one another with breathless speed, when we recall the slow pace of progress in the millennia before the first revolution or even in the four millennia between the second and the Industrial Revolution of modern times.

Between 6000 and 3000 B.C. man has learnt to harness the force of oxen and of winds, he invents the plow, the wheeled cart, and the sailboat, he discovers the chemical processes involved in smelting copper ores and the physical properties of metals, and he begins to work out an accurate solar calendar. He has thereby equipped himself for urban life, and prepares the way for a civilization which shall require writing, processes of reckoning, and standards of measurement—instruments of a new way of transmitting knowledge and of exact sciences. In no period of history till the days of Galileo was progress in knowledge so rapid or far-reaching discoveries so frequent.

The neolithic revolution left the whole area from the Nile and the East Mediterranean across Syria and Iraq to the Iranian plateau and to the Indus valley beyond sprinkled with neolithic communities. It may be assumed that great diversity in culture reigned throughout this vast zone, just as it does to-day. We may suspect many scattered groups of hunters and fishers, survivals of the pre-neolithic economy, migratory horti-culturists, and still more nomadic pastoralists. But none of these communities is as yet directly known; archaeologists have concentrated their attention upon more settled communities, upon the sites of villages which have often grown into cities. Even these exhibit great diversity in crafts, in art, and in general economy, but a few abstract traits are common to all.

The populations are essentially sedentary. The favored sites remain continuously occupied right into historical times. Daughter colonies may be planted as the community grows, but as far as possible the village itself expanded till it became a town. The geographical and economic factors favoring permanent settlement can easily be guessed.

In the first place, really desirable sites are limited in a zone of countries which were becoming increasingly arid and afflicted with ever worse droughts. Permanent water supplies— perennial springs and streams that would supply the needs of large assemblages of men and livestock, and supplement the scanty rainfall by irrigating fields and gardens—were diminishing. As the human race multiplied under the stimulus of the first revolution, such became rare and valuable possessions.

Then the profitable exploitation of these natural oases was a particularly laborious task requiring the collective effort of a large body of workers. Precisely as the ultimate yield in foodstuffs was to be abundant, so the preliminary exertions in preparing the land were heavy and irksome. The Nile, whose annual flood provides both water and soil, offered a certain and abundant livelihood. But the valley bottom that is reached by the flood was originally a series of swamps and reedy jungles. Its reclamation was a stupendous task: the swamps had to be drained by channels, the violence of floodwaters to be restrained by banks, the thicket to be cleared away, the wild beasts lurking in them to be exterminated. No small group could hope to make headway against such obstacles. It needed a strong force capable of acting together to cope with recurrent crises that threatened drainage channels and banks. The few original patches of habitable and cultivable land had to be extended with sweat and blood. The soil, thus hardly conquered, was a sacred heritage; no one would willingly abandon fields so laboriously created. And there was no need to abandon them, since the river itself renewed their fertility every year.

Lower Mesopotamia, the region termed Sumer at the dawn of history, presented a like task. Between the main channels of the Tigris and the Euphrates was a vast tract of swamps, only recently raised by the river silt above the waters of the Persian Gulf. The swamps were covered with a tangle of gigantic reed-brakes interspersed with groves of date-palms. They were interrupted only by low ridges of rocky outcrop or banks of sandy silt. But they swarmed perpetually with animal life while on either side the steppes above flood level were parched and barren throughout the long blazing summer and the bitter winter. Attracted perhaps by the game, wild fowl, and fish, and by the groves of date-palms, the proto-Sumerians tackled the stupendous task of taming the Tigris-Euphrates delta and making it fit for habitation.

The land on which the great cities of Babylonia were to rise had literally to be created; the prehistoric forerunner of the biblical Erech was built on a sort of platform of reeds, laid crisscross upon the alluvial mud. The Hebrew book of Genesis has familiarized us with much older traditions of the pristine condition of Sumer—a "chaos" in which the boundaries between water and dry land were still fluid. An essential incident in "The Creation" is the separation of these elements. Yet it was no god, but the proto Sumerians themselves who created the land; they dug channels to water the fields and drain the marsh; they built dykes and mounded platforms to protect men and cattle from the waters and raise them above the flood; they made the first clearings in the reed brakes and explored the channels between them. The tenacity with which the memory of this struggle persisted in tradition is some measure of the exertion imposed upon the ancient Sumerians. Their reward was an assured supply of nourishing dates, a bounteous harvest from the fields they had drained, and permanent pastures for flocks and herds.

But they would naturally be attached to fields so laboriously won and to settlements so carefully protected: they would not willingly desert them to find new dwellings. And it was easier from the original mound and the nuclear clearing to extend the area of habitable land and cultivate mud than to found fresh settlements in the heart of the undrained swamp. Additional inhabitants were a positive advantage to a marsh village. With their labor, drainage channels could be extended and embankments enlarged to provide more land for cultivation and more room for settlement Even more than in Upper Egypt, natural conditions in Sumer favored a large community and required organized social co-operation on an ever-increasing scale But the same conditions must have prevailed also in the Nile Delta (as contrasted with the narrow valley above Cairo).

In adjacent regions—in the valleys of Syrian or Iranian torrents, for instance—conditions were rather less exacting. But even there permanent improvements had to be effected in the way of irrigation canals and drainage channels, and such would enhance the attraction of the site affected.

So all through the Near East the best sites were reclaimed with toil. Capital in the form of human labor was being sunk in the land. Its expenditure bound men to the soil; they would not lightly forgo the interest brought in by their reproductive works. And all the works in question were collective undertakings, they benefited the community as a whole, and were beyond the power of any individual. And generally their execution required capital in the form of a stock of surplus foodstuffs, accumulated by and at the disposal of the community. The workers engaged in draining and embanking must be fed; but while so employed they were not directly producing the food they consumed. As the reproductive works of a community became more ambitious, so the need for an accumulated stock of surplus foodstuffs would increase. Such an accumulation was a pre-condition of the growth of the village into a city, by conquering ever more of the territory surrounding it from marsh and desert.

Incidentally, conditions of life in a river valley or other oasis place in the hands of society an exceptional power for coercing its members; the community can refuse a recalcitrant access to water and can close the channels that irrigate his fields. Rain falleth upon the just and the unjust alike, but irrigating waters reach the fields by channels that the community has constructed. And what society has provided, society can also withdraw from the unjust and confine to the just alone. The social solidarity needed by irrigators can thus be imposed owing to the very circumstances that demand it. And young men cannot escape the restraint of their elders by founding fresh villages when all beyond the oasis is waterless desert. So when the social will comes to be expressed through a chief or a king, he is invested not merely with moral authority, but with coercive force too; he can apply sanctions against the disobedient.

A third stabilizing factor in the Near East was the enlargement of the farmer's diet: dates, figs, olives, and other fruits were added to barley and wheat-flour. Such fruits are nourishing and easy to preserve and transport. At first they would be gathered from wild trees. A grove of wild date-palms in Sumer or of fig-trees in Syria would enhance the value, and even determine the choice, of a site of settlement. Now fruit-trees go on bearing year after year, but are unmovable. To enjoy their fruits you must abide in their vicinity, or at least return to them every year.

And soon fruit-trees and vines were being cultivated. That, of course, involved an entirely new technique of husbandry. Men had to learn by experience the secrets of pruning for wood or for fruit, of grafting, and of artificial fertilization. The stages of this education are unknown, the beginnings of fruit-growing and viticulture have still to be elucidated. They certainly go back to prehistoric times. Their consequences are obvious. A palm grove or an orchard is a permanent possession in a different sense from a wheatfield. Your sown grain returns you a yield after a few months, but only one crop for each sowing. A date-palm, an olive tree, or a vine returns no fruit for five or more years, but will then go on bearing for perhaps a century. Such permanent plantations inevitably attach their owners to the land far more firmly than fields of wheat or barley. The orchardist is as deeply rooted in the soil as his own precious trees.

Sedentary life gave opportunities for improved housing accommodation and paved the way for architecture. The earliest Egyptian farmers had been content with simple windscreens of reeds plastered with mud. The proto-Sumerians dwelt in tunnel-like houses of growing reeds or of mats hung upon bundles of reeds. But soon houses built of mud or *terre pisée* were being erected both in Egypt and in Asia. And long before 3000 B.C. the brick was invented in Syria or Mesopotamia. It is essentially just a lump of mud mixed with straw, that has been shaped by pressing into a wooden mold and then dried in the sun. But its invention made free construction and monumental architecture possible.

Like pottery, brick put into men's hands a medium of free expression, scarcely restricted as to form or size by the material itself. You have a free choice as to how you shall put your bricks together, just as you have in building up a pot. But the product may now be on a monumental scale. And as such it is no longer an individual creation, but essentially the collective product of many hands.

As in the case of pottery, the first brick buildings kept close to the form of structures in older materials. But even so, in copying in brick the tunnel-like roof of the reed hut, some people in Sumer or Assyria stumbled upon the principle of the true arch; they were applying complicated mechanical laws of thrusts and strains many millennia before these laws had been formulated.

Incidentally, brick architecture quite soon made a contribution to applied mathematics. A brick-stack admirably illustrates the formula for the volume of a parallelepiped. Even though ancient bricks were hardly ever cubes, it was easy to see that the number of bricks in a stack could be found by counting the numbers in three adjacent sides and multiplying these quantities together.

The prosperous farmers settled in the oases and river valleys of the Near East appear to have been much more prone to surrender their economic self-sufficiency than the poor communities that in Europe are styled neolithic. Their readiness to make the sacrifice is a corollary of the variety of economies practiced in the area. As already remarked, besides the prosperous villages of settled farmers, communities of fishers, hunters, and seminomadic pastoralists must be assumed in the intervening spaces. Now the farming communities could easily produce more grain than was needed for home consumption. Very likely they would be glad to part with the surplus in exchange for fish, game, or pastoral products. And the poorer nomads, for their part, would be glad to barter their takings for corn. A certain interdependence between farming villages on the one hand and groups of fishers, hunters, or herdsmen on the other could very easily arise. Such interdependence exists today in a marked degree. The nomad Arab camel-breeders, for instance, depend for grain and manufactures upon settled cultivators. How early the economic specialization of different groups developed into that sort of interdependence is uncertain. It is presupposed in the earliest historical narratives; it may be inferred much earlier. The earliest Egyptian farmers had also been huntsmen, and their weapons were buried with them. In later graves, belonging to the same village, hunting implements are missing. One explanation for their absence would be that the later villagers found it more convenient to barter surplus farm produce for game than to hunt it themselves, as their forefathers had done.

Positive evidence for the gradual breakdown of isolation is afforded by the increasing abundance of imported materials in prehistoric cemeteries and villages. Red Sea and Mediterranean shells have already been recorded in neolithic villages in Egypt. Rather later Egyptian graves contain in addition first malachite and resin, then also lapis lazuli and obsidian; later still amethysts and turquoise appear, and appear in increasing quantities. Now malachite must have been brought from Sinai or the East Desert of Nubia, resin from the forested mountains of Syria or Southern Arabia, obsidian from Melos in the Aegean, Arabia, Armenia, or possibly Abyssinia; lapis lazuli probably from the Iranian plateau.

In Sumer obsidian is found in the oldest settlements together with beads of amazonite that may have been brought from India or at least Armenia. In North Syria and Assyria obsidian was being imported as early as in Sumer, and lapis lazuli and turquoise soon appear. Foreign substances are found as imports very early also at Anau in Russian Turkestan and at Susa in Elam, east of the Tigris.

The transmission of foreign substances over such great distances in the Orient is best explained by the assumption of more mobile populations living alongside the permanent agricultural villages; it would indicate contact between the nomads and the farmers. In any case, it is the beginning of trade, the prerequisite of metallurgy.

The gums and semi-precious stones imported into Sumer and Egypt might be thought to be just luxuries, unessential adjuncts to the toilet. But that would probably be an incorrect judgment; very soon, in any case, these substances came to be regarded as necessities. The Egyptians used malachite for painting their eyelids, and a whole complex of devices grew up around it, as round tobacco-smoking with us. It was carried in richly ornamented leather pouches and ground up on palettes carved into the likeness of animals. The green color counteracted the sun's glare, and copper carbonate acted as a disinfectant against the eye diseases carried by flies in hot countries. But to the Egyptians these effects seemed magical; they valued malachite for the mystic property or *mana* resident in it. That is why its preparation was a ritual, why the pouches were decorated with amulets and the palettes carved into the shape of animals. It was the same with other "imports"—all were regarded as possessing some magic virtue. The cowrie shell resembles the vulva. To wear a cowrie therefore ensured fertility. The shell became a charm. The sanctity thus earned for it has made cowrie shells substitutes for money in parts of Africia and Asia. Native gold and the bright pebbles of the desert—carnelian, opal, and agate—as well as rarer stones, like turquoise and lapis, were again valued not only because they were pretty, but also because magic potencies reside in them. The magic virtues of jewels are frequently mentioned in ancient literatures, and the old ideas persisted throughout the Middle Ages even in Europe. Jewels were thus desired not as mere ornaments, but as practical means to the attainment of success, wealth, long life, offspring. From this standpoint they were not luxuries, but necessaries.

The magic virtue inherent in the substance would be enhanced if it were carved into the likeness of something itself possessing *mana*. If a piece of lapis lazuli were carved in the likeness of a bull, its wearer communicated to himself not only the clarity of the blue sky, but also the potency of a bull. Thus arose the practice of making amulets. It inspired the development of the new and difficult craft of the gem-cutter; the perforation and carving of hard stones for beads and amulets are conspicuous traits common to nearly all the ancient cultures of the Orient, from Crete to Turkestan. It led to the exploitation of glazes. Blue fayence was apparently discovered before the dawn of history. It was not regarded as a substitute for turquoise, but as the result of a magic transmutation of sand and alkali into turquoise—as we might say, synthetic turquoise. It possessed the practical advantage that it could be molded.

Instead of carving the gem into an amulet, its virtue could be enhanced by scratching upon it the representation of some object, or just a magic symbol, like the swastika. Such engraved beads had one peculiar merit: if they were pressed on soft clay, the designs engraved on them would be transferred to the plastic material. This procedure was, of course, a magic operation. Some of the *mana* inherent in the stone was imparted with the symbol. You put your magic on the stamped object. That had the effect of what ethnographers term putting a *tabu* on it; whoever violated it, would be in peril from your magic. And so the engraved stone became a seal. The wad of clay over the mouth of a jar, when stamped with the seal, became a magic guardian of the jar's content. It warned anyone that in breaking the seal he would break a *tabu* and incur magic penalties. Sealing became thereby a means of securing property and asserting ownership. When writing was invented, it would take the place of a signature.

The use of engraved stones as seals is attested from the very earliest neolithic settlements in Assyria. In early times seals were current from the Euphrates eastwards across Iran, while amulets were used instead in Egypt and the Mediterranean coasts. But the two devices quite early began to interpenetrate one another, and a rigid frontier scarcely separated them.

The desire for gold, stones, and shells on account of magic properties supposedly resident in them had important practical consequences. It was a potent factor in breaking down the economic isolation of peasant communities. To obtain magic substances, needed to ensure the fertility of his fields and his own good luck, the thrifty peasant would be ready to part with grains and fruit to the nomads of the desert. To the latter, gems and malachite offered portable articles to barter for agricultural produce. Beads must have formed a staple of the earliest regular trade.

The high estimation of magic substances may well have led to an active search for them. For a later date W. J. Perry has envisaged a worldwide quest for gold, precious stones, amber, and other supposedly magical substances to have been undertaken by the Ancient Egyptians. It would have been a principal factor in the diffusion of civilization. Even though his contention must be regarded as exaggerated, the desire for such substances may well have prompted a sort of geological exploration of regions otherwise uninviting. And one fact is outstanding: malachite is a carbonate of copper, turquoise a phosphate of aluminum tinged with copper; and both occur in connection with copper ores; many of these ores are themselves brightly colored and presumably magical. The collection of malachite, turquoise, and other colored stones accordingly caused men to frequent metalliferous regions and put copper ores into their hands. To this extent the rise of metallurgy that was a dominant factor in the second revolution would be an indirect result of the magical ideas just considered.

Metal working involved two groups or complexes of discoveries: (1) that copper, when hot, melts and can be cast into any desired shape, but on cooling becomes as hard, and will take on as good an edge, as stone, and (2) that the tough, trenchant, reddish metal can be produced by heating certain crystalline stones or earths in contact with charcoal. Copper, indeed, occurs naturally, though only rarely, in the metallic state as native copper. The pre-Columbian Indians of the Great Lakes region in U.S.A. utilized extensive local deposits of native copper for industrial ends. They treated the metal as a superior sort of stone, and even discovered its malleability, producing objects of beaten copper. But they never tried melting and casting it. Their procedures did not lead on to intelligent metallurgy, and it is unlikely that native copper played any significant part in the rise of the industry in the Old World. That depended from the outset on the reduction of copper ores.

The discovery involved might easily be made. A prehistoric Egyptian may have dropped some malachite on the glowing ashes of his hearth and seen the gleaming globules of metallic copper run out. A campfire, lit by some jewel-seeker in a metalliferous district against the outcrop of a surface lode, might reduce some of the ore. In the Katanga district prospectors have noticed beads of copper, thus accidentally smelted, among the ashes of Negroes' campfires. The reduction of copper might be discovered more than once, but its significance need not have been immediately appreciated. Small objects of copper—pins and even harpoon-heads—turn up sporadically in very early Egyptian graves. But they disclose no intelligent realization of the potentialities of metal. The copper has been hammered into thin rods, and bent or beaten into strips, and cut; it has, in fact, been subjected to the processes familiarly applied to bone, stone, and fibers—cutting, hammering, bending.

The real superiority of metal is that it is fusible and can be cast. Fusibility confers upon copper some of the merits of potter's clay. In working it the intelligent artificer is freed from the restrictions of size and shape imposed by bone or stone. A stone axe-head, a flint spear-point, or a bone harpoon can only be made by grinding, chipping, or cutting bits *off* the original piece. Molten copper is completely plastic, and will adapt itself to fill any desired form; it can be run into a mold of any shape and will assume, and on cooling retain, precisely the form outlined by the mold. The only limit to size is the capacity of the mold; you can run into it as much copper as you like. And the molds themselves can be made of potter's clay, the potentialities of which were considered on p. 76.

On the other hand, though so plastic when hot, the metal on cooling possesses the essential virtues of stone and bone; it is as solid, and will take as sharp an edge or as fine a point. Yet it has the additional advantage of being malleable. And finally, it is more permanent than stone or bone. A stone axe may easily be splintered by hard usage, and is then done for; at best its edge will often need regrinding, and it will soon be reduced to a useless size. But a copper axe can be remelted again and again, and will come out as good as new. The intelligent use of metal—let us say, simply metallurgy—begins when these advantages have been realized.

But that realization required a readjustment of the forms of thought. The change from tough solid copper to molten metal and back to the solid state again is dramatic, and must have seemed mysterious. The sameness between the shapeless lump of raw copper, the liquid in the crucible, and the well-formed casting, must at first have been difficult to grasp. Man was here controlling a remarkable process of physical change. He would have to adjust whatever naïve ideas of substance he entertained in order to recognize identity through its several stages.

Moreover, the control of the process was only possible by means of a whole complex of discoveries and inventions. A temperature in the neighborhood of $1200°$ C. is requisite to melt copper. That requires a blast. Some device had to be invented for forcing a current of air upon the flame; bellows are the correct solution, but are not directly attested till 1600 B.C. Furnaces, crucibles, and tongs had to be invented. Casting requires molds. It is easy enough to reproduce by casting an object that is flat on one side by impressing it on clay and pouring molten metal in the hollow left by the pattern. But that is useless for making a stout dagger with a ridge on both faces to strengthen it. Such an implement required a two-piece mold, the halves of which must correspond exactly and must be bound or clamped together. By 3000 B.C. the ingenious *cire perdue* process was employed in Mesopotamia. A model of the desired object is first made in wax and then coated in clay; the clay is heated, becoming pottery, while the wax is allowed to run out; metal is then poured into the cavity, and finally the clay mold is broken, disclosing the metal casting reproducing the form of the wax model.

These few words may suggest how intricate the course of casting really is. But the actual operations are much more tedious and intricate than a page of print can indicate. For instance, precautions must be taken to prevent the liquid metal from oxidizing or sticking to the mold. In a closed mold there is a danger of air bubbles forming, which would cause a fatal weakness in the casting. Again, after casting, the tool has to be hammered and smoothed down with a file or an abrasive.

Evidently the smith must dispose of a formidable body of industrial lore; his craft traditions embody the results of long experience and many deliberate experiments. They represent a new branch of applied science—elements carried over into modern chemistry and physics—but blended with a tangle of magic that we have happily forgotten. The transmission of this lore need not differ in kind from that of potter's lore. But the smith's task was more complicated and exacting than hers, the knowledge he required more specialized. It is very doubtful whether metallurgy could be practiced as a domestic industry in the intervals of agricultural work. Among modern barbarians smiths are normally specialists, and metal-working has probably always been a full-time job. The smith's may therefore be the oldest specialized craft save the magician's. But a community can afford a smith only if it possesses a surplus of foodstuffs; the smith, being withdrawn from food-production himself, must be fed from the unconsumed surplus of the farmers. The industrial use of metal may thus be treated as a sign of the specialization of labor, that a community's food supply exceeds its normal needs.

But it generally means more; it usually means the final sacrifice of economic independence. Copper is far from common; its ores are not found on the alluvial and löss plains preferred by neolithic farmers, but among wooded or stony ranges. Very few farming communities can have possessed copper mines on their home territory; the great majority had always to import the metal or its ore. In the end it had to be obtained by the production of a surplus of foodstuffs above what was needed for home consumption.

The scientific and economic implications of the extraction of metal from its ores are perhaps more far-reaching than those of metal-working. Copper ores are crystalline or powdery minerals generally occurring as veins in hard ancient rocks. The transformation of the ores into copper is a fairly simple chemical change. But what an astonishing one to early man! The ore does not look the least like the metal. The change it undergoes in contact with glowing carbon is miraculous—surely a change of substance, a transsubstantiation! The recognition of a continuity of substance must have been been very difficult, and a rational account was achieved only by modern chemistry; till then alchemical ideas about transmutation could subsist. But, whatever his theories, man learned enough practical chemistry to distinguish what sorts of stone would yield copper when heated with carbon.

The right sorts of stone are, as remarked, far from common. Once alive to the value of metal and the possibility of transmuting stones into it, men must have sought deliberately for suitable ores and made numerous experiments, trying first one stone and then another. Many were fruitless, but other metals were discovered in the quest. Silver and lead both occur in prehistoric graves in Egypt, and were extensively used in Mesopotamia before 3000 B.C. Beads of meteoric iron occur in Egyptian graves shortly before 3000 B.C., and a little later iron ores were occasionally smelted in Mesopotamia. But on an industrial scale iron was not smelted nor worked anywhere before 1400 B.C. Tin was known to the metallurgists of Sumer and the Indus valley soon after 3000 B.C., being employed chiefly as an alloy of copper to simplify the process of casting.

The first copper ores to be exploited were presumably derived from surface deposits. Many such lodes must once have existed, but have been exhausted long before modern geological surveys were started. Eventually, however, men had to follow the vein beneath the ground and begin mining. The copper miner had to learn how to split hard rocks by kindling fires against them and throwing water on the heated surfaces. Systems of propping and timbering had to be devised to support the walls and roofs of the galleries. The ore had to be broken up, separated from the rock by washing, and transported to the surface. No records, however, survive to illustrate the steps by which the science of mining was founded; but by 1000 B.C. copper miners, even in still-barbarous Europe, were applying a science that a layman today can admire, but cannot attempt to expound.

The art of smelting is no less abstruse. As in casting, some sort of a blast is essential. And for production on a large scale a furnace had to be devised. And only surface ores of copper can be directly reduced by heating with charcoal; deeper ores are generally sulphides, and have to be roasted in the open to oxidize them before they can be smelted. Other metals require different treatment. Lead, for example, will volatilize and vanish with the smoke if its ore be heated in the sort of open furnace used for smelting copper.

Prospectors, miners, and smelters must therefore command a body of knowledge even more abstruse than that demanded of the smith. They must have classified the different kinds of ore, learned the outward signs for their diagnosis, the appropriate techniques for their treatment. The requisite knowledge could only be gained by experimentation and comparison of results on an even larger scale than was demanded by metalworking. Mining must have been an even more specialized trade than that of the smith. Miners as a rule cannot have been food-producers, but must have relied on a surplus of foodstuffs produced by those who consumed their products.

Intelligent metallurgy must have been widely understood in the Ancient East soon after 4000 B.C. But metal ousted stone very slowly. The advantages, stressed above, must not be exaggerated. For hoeing up the soil, stone blades serve the cultivator well; he will often have to replace them, but normally that is easy. A flint blade works excellently for cutting up carcasses, for reaping grains, for trimming leather, and even for shaving; it wears out quickly, but a new knife or razor can be fashioned in a few minutes where flint is abundant. Stone axes or adzes will fell trees, shape posts, or hew out a canoe almost as quickly and neatly as copper ones; only you will have to pause periodically and make a new axe from a convenient pebble. The chief defect of stone tools was that they wore out so quickly. But when the raw materials were lying about and time was not absurdly precious, it was not an intolerable hardship to have to make new tools from time to time. It needed the special geographical conditions of an alluvial plain, where suitable stones were rare, to drive home the value of the new and more permanent material and to create an effective and general demand for metal. And to make the satisfaction of that demand possible, improved methods of transport were needed. That meant the harnessing of animal motive power and of the winds. Both were, like the discovery of metal and the invention of metallurgy, preconditions of the second revolution and achieved before it.

Harnessing the strength of oxen or asses and the forces of the wind was man's first effective essay in making natural force work for him. When he had succeeded, he found himself for the first time controlling and even directing continuous forces not supplied by his own muscles. He was on the right road to releasing his body from the more brutal forms of physical labor—the road that leads to the internal-combustion engine and the electric motor, the steam hammer and the mechanical navvy. And at the same time he was learning new principles in mechanics and physics.

Mixed farmers had a suitable motive power ready to hand in the cattle they had already domesticated. Perhaps the ox was first set to drawing a plow. But, of course, a plow had to be invented—the long-bladed hoe of the prehistoric Egyptians, the draw-spade such as is still used in Japan, or a foot-plow like those used in the Hebrides last century may have provided the model. And the plow heralded an agricultural revolution. Plowing stirs up those fertile elements in the soil that in semi-arid regions are liable to sink down beyond the reach of plant roots. With two oxen and a plow a man can cultivate in a day a far larger area than can a woman with a hoe. The plot gives place to the field, and agriculture (from Latin *ager,* "a field") really begins. And all that means larger crops, more food, and expanding population. And incidentally men replace women as principals in cultivation. When this revolution was accomplished is quite unknown. In Hither Asia, Egypt, and the Aegean it had been completed long before the dawn of history. But in Germany the cultivation of small plots with hoes was still the sole economy down to about 2000 B.C.

In open desert and steppe country the ox could be made to draw a sledge or travoise such as primitive hunting tribes still use for the transport of tents and furniture from camp to camp. (The dog having attached himself to man long before cattle or sheep were domesticated, dog-sleighs may be older than ox-carts and sledges.) Ox-drawn sledges were still being used about 3000 B.C. at Ur to convey to their final resting place royal corpses. But long before that date the sledge had been transformed by an invention that revolutionized locomotion on land. The wheel was the crowning achievement of prehistoric carpentry; it is the precondition of modern machinery, and, applied to transport, it converted the sledge into a cart or wagon—the direct ancestor of the locomotive and the automobile.

It is easy enough to make guesses as to how the wheel might have been invented, but reliable data on the subject are hard to obtain. As wooden objects cannot normally last many centuries, the archaeologist can only learn about vehicles from people who happen to have left drawings or models of them in some durable material like pottery or stone. Their admittedly defective and one-sided testimony justifies the following positive statements: Wheeled vehicles are represented in Sumerian art as early as 3500 B.C., and in North Syria perhaps even earlier. By 3000 B.C. carts, wagons, and even chariots were in general use in Elam, Mesopotamia, and Syria. In the Indus valley wheeled carts were in use when the archaeological record begins about 2500 B.C., and at about the same date in Turkestan too. Some five centuries later, at least, they are attested in Crete and Asia Minor. On the other hand, the device was definitely not used by the Egyptians till about 1650 B.C., when it was forced upon them by Asiatic invaders, the Hyksos.

FIG. 5.—PLOWING, MILKING, AND HOEING IN ANCIENT EGYPT.

The earliest wheeled vehicles were naturally clumsy affairs. Even by 3000 B.C. the Sumerian chariots and wagons had solid wheels composed of three pieces of wood clamped together and bound with leather tires studded with copper nails. The wheels turned in one piece with the axle, which was fastened underneath the car's body with leather straps. The village ox-carts in Sindh today faithfully repeat this structure.

The wheel not only revolutionized transport, it was already applied in manufacturing industry by 3500 B.C., and a brief digression is needed to explain this. With a horizontal wheel, at the center of which he can set his lump of clay spinning, the potter can shape in a couple of minutes a vessel that it would take several days to build up by hand. And the product will be more symmetrical. Pot-making was the first mechanized industry, the first to apply the wheel to manufacturing machinery. And the craft was transformed as a result. Ethnography shows that among the simpler people today the making of pots by hand is a domestic craft plied by the women, whereas manufacture on the wheel is a specialized trade reserved to men. The available evidence suggests that the same was true of antiquity. And so the introduction of the wheel into the ceramic industry marks another step in the specialization of labor; the potters are now specialists, withdrawn from the primary task of food-production and exchanging their wares for a share in the communal surplus.

These two primary uses of the wheel may just possibly have arisen independently, though that is scarcely credible. In any case, they do not always go together. In Hither Asia and

FIG. 6.—EARLY SUMERIAN WAR CHARIOT.

India, indeed, wheel-made pots are certainly as old as wheeled vehicles. But in Egypt the potters' wheel was adopted before the wheeled car, whereas in Crete models of wagons are a couple of centuries older than the earliest wheel-turned pots. In Europe the potters' wheel was not employed north of the Alps till after 500 B.C., though wheeled vehicles had been in use perhaps a thousand years earlier. But this is, after all, a digression.

The introduction of wheeled vehicles drawn by oxen or other beasts accelerated communications and enormously simplified the transportation of goods. Vehicles do not, however, represent the sole method of employing animal motive

power in transportation. Goods can be loaded directly on a
beast's back and men can sit there. About 2000 B.C. merchandise was normally carried between Babylonia and Asia Minor
on donkey-back. The history of this sort of transport is even
harder to decipher in the archaeological record than is that
of vehicular traffic. The donkey is native to Northeast Africa,
and must have been domesticated there long before 3000 B.C.,
presumably to act as a beast of burden. Tame asses are recorded in Egypt by the date just mentioned, and at the same time
were being employed to draw plows in Mesopotamia. Thereafter the ass remains the commonest beast of burden and
riding-animal in the Near East.

The horse too, Forde thinks, may have been domesticated
first for milking and riding. But apart from some dubious
models of saddles from the Indus valley, dating round about
2500 B.C., there is no really satisfactory evidence for horse-
riding much before 1000 B.C. The beast is supposed to be a
native of the steppes of Central Asia and Europe. In Hither
Asia horses certainly appear about 2000 B.C., and were introduced thence into Egypt by the Hyksos about 1650 B.C. But
in all cases they appear exclusively as draught animals har-
nessed to war-chariots. And at a still earlier date, 3000 B.C. or
before, some sort of equid is depicted drawing chariots on
Sumerian monuments. The identity of these beasts is, however,
disputed. Some authorities, such as Frankfort, say the animal
is meant for a horse; others say a mule; the majority, including
Hilzheimer and Woolley, now contend that an onager—the
Asiatic wild ass—is intended. It should be remarked in parenthesis that the harness used in connection with the Sumerian
and all other ancient chariots seems to be modeled on that
originally devised for attaching the bullock to a cart. And
owing to the anatomical differences between bovids and
equids, this ancient harness was very burdensome to horses,
and consequently very inefficient.

None the less the domestication of horses must have sub-
stantially increased the range and speed of communication.
Even though this acceleration would seem, on the available
evidence, to fall largely outside the period surveyed in this
chapter, horse transport has to be reckoned with as a possibility before the second revolution: there may have been
peoples on the edge of the well-explored valley tracts, already
endowed with the mobility that the control of horses guaran-
tees. Such hypothetical peoples may have acted as agents in
the diffusion of ideas and inventions over distances and with
speeds inconceivable if bullock-carts and donkeys had been
the fastest means of conveyance available. And another possi-

bility must be remembered: camels or dromedaries may have been tamed before 3000 B.C. But, given camels, deserts cease to be barriers to intercourse and become, like seas, links between centers of population.

Parallel with the foregoing improvements in land transport went developments in navigation. But the evidence is even more scanty than that just surveyed. Dugout canoes and skinboats must have been used by fishers before the first revolution. Soon after it paintings on prehistoric Egyptian vases disclose substantial boats made of bundles of papyrus lashed together, propelled by forty or more rowers or paddlers, and equipped with a sort of cabin near the center. But sailboats are not depicted in Egypt till a little after 3500 B.C., and seem to belong to a type foreign to the Nile. Yet it is almost certain that by 3000 B.C. at latest sailboats were freely navigating the eastern Mediterranean. Though there is even less direct evidence, the same statement would surely apply to the Arabian Sea too.

Thus men have begun to overcome the mechanical difficulties in the way of marine transport (they have, that is, learned to build plank boats and to rig sails), and have acquired sufficient topographical and astronomical knowledge to utilize the highways of the sea. By water, as by land, the people of the Orient were now in a position to pool their natural resources and the experience they were severally building up.

The arts, processes, and contrivances just enumerated are outward expressions of a body of science and applications of accumulated experience. Their diffusion means also the pooling of that practical knowledge. It equipped the peoples of the Orient with the technical control over Nature requisite for the completion of a second revolution, the establishment of a new type of economy and society. But other factors intervened before the knowledge thus acquired was applied in actual practice.

The vast area between the Nile and the Ganges has in the foregoing pages been treated very much as a unit, despite insistence on diversity of economies within it; the developments just traced have been presented as a continuous and peaceful process. But such an account hardly corresponds to the archaeological facts. Radical and sometimes catastrophic changes in pottery and domestic architecture, in art and burial rites, are in reality discernible in the settlement mounds of Iran, Mesopotamia, and Syria, and in the cemeteries of Egypt. Such changes are generally held to indicate displacements of population, the conquest or invasion by and infiltration of new peoples.

In a region exposed to droughts and floods, migrations are liable to happen, especially when its inhabitants are utterly dependent on Nature for crops and fodder. A sudden drought then may mean starvation for peasants relying on dry cultivation and for pastoralists grazing their herds on the steppe. And the specter of famine may drive its victims to seek food in the river valleys where grain for men and fodder for stock are still obtainable; they may enter as suppliants, like the "Children of Israel," and accept some sort of servitude in exchange for life, or they may find refuge in force of arms and arrive as conquerors. In any case, the steppe-folk thus set in motion will mix with, replace, or dominate the older valley population.

The changes in material culture, art, and religion reflected in the archaeological record of the Orient must in many cases have been due precisely to immigrations and conquests of the sort just adumbrated, and books on Oriental prehistory are largely preoccupied with the attempt to define and trace the movements of peoples thus revealed. But here it is enough to remind the reader that evidence for such migration actually exists, and then to suggest certain consequences for the growth of human economy.

It is believed that the "clash of cultures" set up by invasion and immigration facilitates the spread of new ideas by breaking down the rigidity of established societies. To survive, any society must attain an adjustment to its environment; it lives by exploiting the natural resources of its territory. But just in so far as the adjustment achieved is successful, the community concerned will tend to become conservative. When a group are enjoying a sufficiency of food in simple comfort with spells of rest, why should they change their behavior? They have painfully learned the tricks and dodges, the arts and crafts necessary to coax this modicum of prosperity out of Nature; why do more? Indeed, change may be dangerous. The success of simply equipped societies depends on everyone doing what has proved to be the right thing at the right time and in the proper way; it imposes a complete pattern of behavior on all the community's members. This pattern finds expression in social institutions and in traditional rules and prohibitions. It is sanctified by magico-religious beliefs and fears. Just as the practical acts of life are accompanied by appropriate rites and ceremonies, so mystical forces are supposed to watch over the traditional rules and avenge any transgression of them. The established economy is reinforced by an appropriate ideology.

The force of superstitions that consolidate and maintain established social institutions and economic arrangements is enormous in the simpler societies of today. It must have been so too in the Ancient East. The adjustment then achieved by even the most favored communities was, after all, very precarious. An insufficient or an excessive flood, an untimely hailstorm, a plague of locusts, might imperil the whole community; for its resources were restricted, its reserves were small. But the disasters threatening its life are mysterious and even today incalculable. They might very easily be regarded as supernatural interventions, inflicted to avenge transgressions of customary rules of behavior. Any divergence from established practice, any departure from behavior that had been found safe and effective, might theoretically provoke such punishments. Any innovation was therefore dangerous, and public opinion would frown upon change.

But if an immigrant community mingle with the old, this complacent and timid conservatism will be disturbed. The new arrivals have *ex hypothesi* grown up under different conditions; they will accordingly have created for themselves an economy appropriate to their own environment. They feel needs different from, and perhaps complementary to, those experienced by the older inhabitants. For instance, if pastoralists, they may be accustomed to eat more meat than is usually consumed by peasants. They may have come to prize obsidian for the manufacture of knives, and so be dissatisfied with flint which is less delicate. Or they may regard substances—lapis lazuli, for instance—that had been easily obtainable in their original territory, as indispensable. New demands will thus be added to the old by the new arrivals.

Again the newcomers will bring their own institutions and their own ideology. The prescriptions and prohibitions, the rites and ceremonies, regarded as essential to life in their former environment, are not likely to coincide entirely with those respected by the original inhabitants of the occupied territory. Two patterns of behavior, two sets of institutions, two bodies of ideas will thus be operating side by side and competitively. It may thus be demonstrated to both parties that departures from traditional modes of action, regarded by one or other as obligatory, are not so dangerous, after all. The land still yields its fruit, though turned over with a plow guided by men instead of a hoe wielded by women.

Finally, it has been suggested that conquest is an essential prerequisite to the accumulation of communal capital needed for the accomplishment of the second revolution. The latter required that a substantial proportion of the community should be permanently withdrawn from the primary business of getting food to be employed by reproductive works, in secondary industries, in transportation, commerce, and administration. That is possible only if there is a surplus of foodstuffs already available to support those members of the community who are no longer themselves producing their own food. Moreover, in practice a surplus is needed to barter for raw materials not available locally.

Now the farmers in the Nile Valley or Mesopotamia could easily produce the requisite surplus. They would, indeed, doubtless produce so much above their immediate needs as to provide against bad seasons. But why should they do more? Man, it is argued, is a lazy beast and prefers a simple life to luxuries earned by unremitting toil. Conquest would certainly constitute one means of overcoming this natural inertia. A tribe of pastoralists, for instance, may conquer the land of a peasant community. They will leave the peasants on the land, and even protect them from other enemies, on condition that they pay a tribute of farm produce. The peasant is thereby obliged to exert himself to produce more than he needs for the support of his own household; he must provide a substantial share, perhaps more than he retains himself, for his new "masters." These form a sort of landed "aristocracy," a class living off the tribute of peasants. The system is familiar; it survives in a very simple form in East Africa; it was characteristic of medieval Europe and was widespread in antiquity.

Now such an "aristocracy" is generally also an oligarchy; its members are far less numerous than the peasants who remain the primary producers. Yet the landlords can extort from these far more farm produce than they can themselves consume. They thus dispose of an abundant surplus of foodstuffs, part of which they will employ for the support of workers producing manufactured articles, which aristocrats can consume, and for foreign trade.

Now it must be admitted that the realization of the second revolution did require an accumulation of capital in the form primarily of foodstuffs, that the accumulation had to some extent to be concentrated to make it effectively available for social ends, and that in Egypt the first accumulation and concentration was apparently the result of conquest. But it is not demonstrable that such conquest was in all cases the effective cause for the necessary accumulation and concentration of capital. In Mesopotamia we shall see that it was nominally a native god (in practice, of course, the corporation of his self-appointed priests) that administered the accumulated wealth of a Sumerian city; there are only the vaguest and most ambiguous hints of an aristocracy owing its wealth to conquest rather than to religious prestige and home-grown social tradition. And in the oldest Indian cities we simply do not know how the communal surplus was accumulated or controlled. Military conquest is one means of assuring the accumulation of a surplus of wealth. But theories that regard it as an essential precondition of the second revolution must be regarded with reserve.

Other corollaries to the disturbances of peaceful development at which the archaeological record hints are better attested. On the site of one village we find another, the arrangement, architecture, and furniture of which are so different from those of its predecessor as to indicate a real break in the social tradition; that must mean the arrival of a new people to replace or dominate the former settlers. But such replacement or domination can hardly have taken place peacefully. It must surely have been achieved by force, *i.e.* by war. In that case some sort of warfare must have been waged before the second revolution was consummated.

This has, of course, been denied by Elliot Smith and Perry, and it is not easy to prove warfare by archaeological evidence. Weapons are, of course, found in graves and settlements that are older than the revolution. But it is not easy to distinguish weapons of war from implements of the chase, arms for killing men from those for dispatching game. Again, very early settlements—for instance at Susa—were certainly protected by some sort of ramparts. Most probably these were defenses against human foes, but they might conceivably have been designed merely to keep out marauding wild beasts. On the whole, warlike raids by nomadic or uprooted peoples have to be admitted. And if so, it is equally necessary to admit some degree of organized defenses against such raiders on the part of the prosperous settled communities. In a word, warfare has to be admitted though only on a small scale and of a spasmodic kind. Yet it might be an industry. Cattle and grain stolen from peasants supported life just as well as those you reared or grew yourself. The protection of crops and herds against marauders was just as vital a part of the communal economy as sowing the fields and breeding cattle.

Now, warfare must have economic repercussions. More than anything else, perhaps, it stimulated the demand for metal. It does not matter much if a flint knife breaks in skinning an animal. It is a much more serious matter if the accident happens in hand-to-hand combat with an enemy. It was battle, above all, that manifested the superiority of tough durable copper or bronze over brittle flint and stone. Again, warfare gave exceptional opportunities for outstanding individuals to display courage and capacity for leadership, and thus to earn prestige and authority. It thus became a contributory factor in the rise of chiefs invested with effective temporal power, and ultimately of monarchs.

Finally, war helped to a great discovery—that men as well as animals can be domesticated. Instead of killing a defeated enemy, he might be enslaved; in return for his life he could be made to work. This discovery has been compared in importance to that of the taming of animals. In any case, by early historic times slavery was a foundation of ancient industry and a potent instrument in the accumulation of capital. Bound captives, presumably doomed to servitude, are depicted on some of the oldest figured documents (sealings) from Mesopotamia, and are as ancient as scenes of battle.

But war was not necessarily the sole source of slaves. The poorer or weaker members of a community might surrender their services to more prosperous fellows in return for food or shelter. Exiles from another community might be accepted on the same terms. Whole communities of refugees from drought might be allowed to settle in valleys and oases in return for dues or services; the "Children of Israel" are by no means the only Asiatic tribe known from contemporary records to have found refuge in Egypt under such conditions. The recruitment of slaves or clients by other means than capture is illustrated among various barbarian and savage peoples of modern times, and is suggested by quite early written texts. War and famine were alike potential agents recruiting the labor force at the disposal of cities after the second revolution. The great public works then undertaken, the variety of crafts thereafter plied, employed a host of workers. The latters' status is hard to define. How many labored "freely" in return for wages, or out of sheer piety, or like conscripts in fulfilment of customary obligations to the community, or finally as slaves, the absolute chattels of an individual, a temple, or a State? All we know for the earliest times is that every laborer who continued to work must somehow be fed and supported by the surplus gathered by primary producers.

And over against the possible slaves we have to reckon with privileged classes—indeed, with chiefs or even kings. The Egyptians preserved explicit traditions of independent dynasties ruling in Upper and Lower Egypt before the unification of the land under one sovereign, the first Pharaoh, Menes, originally a king of Upper Egypt. But this unification seems to coincide with the realization of the second revolution in

Egypt. In that case we must admit kings in Egypt before the revolution. The same inference may perhaps be drawn from Sumerian traditions of dynasties ruling "before the Flood," whatever that may mean. In any case, a way to royal power must have been open before city life began. Conquest was not the sole road to a throne—economic success, but most of all magico-religious prestige, might lead to that glory. The magician may have been the first independent craftsman, the first member of any community to have a claim on the surplus product of the collective food-quest without contributing thereto by physical activity. But the magician's wand is an embryo scepter, and historical kings still retain many trappings from their magic office.

Now the first revolution had not abolished magic. Quite the reverse. Man, let us insist again, was still dependent on the incalculable chances of rain, flood, sunshine, still exposed to disaster from droughts, earthquakes, hailstorms, and other natural but unpredictable catastrophes. He still sought to control the beneficent forces and to ward off noxious powers by rituals, incantations, and charms. Anyone who could successfully claim to control the elements by his magic would, of course, earn immense prestige and authority. It is needless to demonstrate in detail how many opportunities of aggrandizement through alleged magical prowess must have presented themselves in ancient societies, but the chapter may be fitly closed with a reference to one great discovery: that of the solar calendar—that on one theory was one of the sources of royal authority in Egypt.

Farming in the Nile Valley is entirely dependent upon the annual flood; the latter's advent is the signal for the whole cycle of agricultural operations to start. To forecast precisely the day of its arrival and warn the peasant to prepare for it, would be and is of great advantage to all the valley's population. It would at the same time seem to be a proof of some sort of supernatural knowledge and power; the distinction between prediction and control is too subtle for simple peoples. Yet in reality the forecast can be made with considerable precision. The flood is a function of the annual movement of the earth round the sun—actually it depends upon the southwest monsoon breaking upon the mountains of Abyssinia. It will normally reach any given place at the same point in each of the earth's journeys round the sun—that is, on the same day in each solar year. All that is necessary, therefore, is to know the length of the solar year and reckon such a year from one observed flood as starting-point to the next.

Now most simple people who have any sort of calendar at

all reckon by lunar months, and not by solar years, and there is evidence that the Egyptians were no exception to the rule. But no fixed number of lunar months (lunations) corresponds exactly to a solar year. To be able to predict the flood, therefore, the Egyptians had to determine the length of the solar year in days and devise an artificial calendar to reconcile solar and lunar years. Now observations recorded over a period of fifty years would suffice to show that the average interval between inundations was, to the nearest day, 365 days. On this basis an official calendar was introduced, most probably at the time of the unification of Egypt under Menes, in which the year of 365 days was divided into ten months of thirty-six days each, with a period of five intercalary days each year. It is difficult to see how even this result could have been obtained without written records, and it represents the first triumph of mathematical astronomy and the first vindication of the claim of science to predict. But of course there was an error in the calculation of just under six hours, and the accumulation of this error in time put the calendar entirely out of gear with the real seasons, and made it useless as a guide to the peasants in their agricultural work. New Year's Day originally coincided with the advent of the inundation, but after a century the inundation could not be expected until the 25th day of the first month. The royal officials discovered how to correct this error by observations on the star Sirius (Egyptian: Sothis) which, in the latitude of Cairo, is the last star to appear on the horizon before dawn obscures all stars at the flood season. They used their observations on the "heliacal rising" of Sirius to give the signal for the start of agricultural operations, but by this time it was too late to reform the official calendar—the requisite reform would have aroused the same sort of opposition, but naturally much more bitter, as has frustrated all attempts to fix the date of Easter. So the old official calendar was maintained, though the Egyptians recognized as Sothic cycles the periods of 1461 years when the official New Year's Day did actually coincide with the heliacal rising of Sirius.

Now historical kings in Egypt, as in Babylonia and elsewhere, were intimately connected with the regulation of the calendar. It has been suggested that they owed their authority in part at least to that first application of predictive science, the establishment of the calendar. The Pharaohs may even have kept secret the further discovery of the utility of the heliacal rising of Sirius as a sign of the flood's proximity to exploit it for their own prestige. The knowledge would have enabled the Pharaoh to predict the flood to the fellahin, and thus vindicate his magical powers of controlling the seasons and the crops. That is perhaps just a nice speculation. The determination of the solar year and the creation of an official calendar dependent on that standard are historical facts of the highest importance for the history of science. For the Egyptian is admittedly the parent of all Old World solar calendars, including our own.

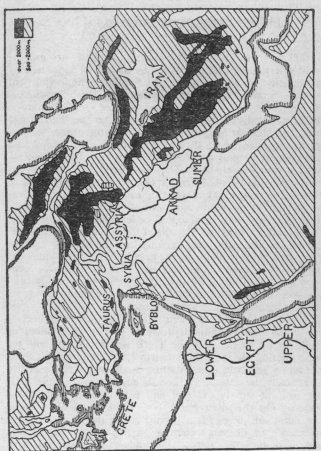

Fig. 7.—Sketch Map of the Cradles of Civilization.

CHAPTER VII

THE URBAN REVOLUTION

By 4000 B.C. the great tract of semi-arid lands around the East Mediterranean and eastwards to India was populated by a multiplicity of communities. Among them a diversity of economies, appropriate to the variety of local conditions, must be imagined—hunters and fishers, hoe-cultivators, nomadic pastoralists, and settled farmers. And on their fringe we can add other tribes spreading out into the distant wilderness. Among them these diverse communities had augmented man's cultural capital by the discoveries and inventions indicated in the last chapter. They had severally accumulated an imposing body of scientific knowledge—topographical, geological, astronomical, chemical, zoological, and botanical —of practical craftlore on agriculture, mechanics, metallurgy, and architecture, and of magical beliefs that might also enshrine scientific truths. As a result of the commerce and movements of peoples just hinted at, such science, techniques, and beliefs were being widely diffused; knowledge and skill were being pooled. And at the same time the exclusiveness of local groups was being broken down, the rigidity of social institutions was being relaxed, self-sufficing communities were sacrificing their economic independence.

The last-named development progressed faster than elsewhere in the great riverine depressions, in the Nile Valley, on the alluvial plains between the Tigris and Euphrates, and on those bordering the Indus and its tributaries in Sindh and Punjab. There a generous and unfailing water supply and a fertile soil annually renewed by floods ensured a reliable and superabundant supply of food and permitted the population to expand. On the other hand, both the original draining of the marshes and jungles fringing the rivers and the subsequent maintenance of drainage channels and protective dykes imposed exceptionally heavy demands for sustained and disciplined effort upon the communities profiting by these advantages. And, as explained on p. 90, irrigation placed in the communities' hand an effective means of enforcing discipline.

And, despite the abundance of foodstuffs, alluvial valleys

are exceptionally poor in other raw materials essential to civilized life. The Nile Valley lacked timber for building, free-stone, ores, and magic stones. Sumer was still worse off. The only native timber was supplied by the date-palm, quarries of building stone were remoter and less accessible than in Egypt; not only was copper ore lacking, but flint of which the Nile cliffs furnished an excellent supply was equally hard to obtain. Indeed, on the alluvial plains and marshes even hard pebbles, suitable for making axeheads, were rarities. From the very first the Sumerians had had to import Armenian obsidian or other exotic stones for cutting tools. Sindh and Punjab suffered from the same shortage of essential raw materials as Sumer.

And so on the large alluvial plains and riverside flatlands the need for extensive public works to drain and irrigate the land and to protect the settlement would tend to consolidate social organization and to centralize the economic system. At the same time, the inhabitants of Egypt, Sumer, and the Indus basin were forced to organize some regular system of trade or barter to secure supplies of essential raw materials. The fertility of lands gave their inhabitants the means for satis-fying their need of imports. But economic self-sufficiency had to be sacrificed and a completely new economic structure created. The surplus of home-grown products must not only suffice to exchange for exotic materials; it must also support a body of merchants and transport workers engaged in obtain-ing these and a body of specialized craftsmen to work the precious imports to the best advantage. And soon soldiers would be needed to protect the convoys and back up the merchants by force, scribes to keep records of transactions growing ever more complex, and State officials to reconcile conflicting interests.

And so by 3000 B.C. the archaeologist's picture of Egypt, Mesopotamia, and the Indus valley no longer focuses atten-tion on communities of simple farmers, but on States em-bracing various professions and classes. The foreground is occupied by priests, princes, scribes, and officials, and an army of specialized craftsmen, professional soldiers, and miscellaneous laborers, all withdrawn from the primary task of food-production. The most striking objects now unearthed are no longer the tools of agriculture and the chase and other products of domestic industry, but temple furniture, weapons, wheel-made pots (p. 102), jewelry, and other manufactures turned out on a large scale by skilled artisans. As monuments we have instead of huts and farmhouses, monumental tombs, temples, palaces, and workshops. And in them we find all manner of exotic substances, not as rarities, but regularly imported and used in everyday life.

Evidently the change in the archaeologists' material reflects a transformation in the economy that produced the material. Evidently too the transformation should be accompanied by a rise in the population. Priests, officials, merchants, artisans, and soldiers should represent new classes that, as classes, could find no livelihood in a self-sufficing food-producing community, still less in a band of hunters. And the archaeological evidence alone suffices to confirm that expectation. The new cities are spatially larger and can accomodate a much denser population than the agricultural villages that have been absorbed in them or that still subsist beside them. Mohenjo-daro in Sindh, for example, spread over a square mile of land; it was a close agglomeration of two-storied houses neatly arranged along broad streets or narrow alleys. Again, the urban cemeteries attest not only an increase of wealth, but also multiplication of people. On the Nile we have not only village graveyards continuing from prehistoric times, but also large cemeteries of monumental tombs reserved for royalties and officials. The so-called "royal cemetery" at Ur was probably used by only a fraction of the citizen body, and on the most generous estimate for not more than three centuries (most authorities would reduce this figure by half). Yet it comprised over 700 interments still recognizable when discovered—a vastly larger number than found in any purely prehistoric cemetery.

The change from self-sufficing food-production to an economy based also on specialized manufacture and external trade did accordingly promote a marked expansion of the population. It had such an effect on vital statistics as to earn the title of revolution on the definition given on p. 19.

In the economic sphere the results of the second revolution in Egypt, Mesopotamia, and India were similar, but only in an abstract way. Concretely its results were strikingly different in each area. The details not only of the economic structures but also of the political and religious systems reposing thereon diverge conspicuously. This divergence extends down to the simplest archaeological objects. In each region smiths were working the same chemical substances by analogous simple processes into tools and weapons to serve common human needs. But their products—axes, knives, daggers and spearheads—assume quite distinct forms on the Nile, on the Euphrates, and on the Indus. There is no less contrast between Indian, Sumerian and Egyptian pottery, though the potter's craft was common to the three regions. And like contrasts can be followed in every aspect of man's activity. An abstract account of the revolution in general cannot therefore take the place of a description of its course in the several regions.

In Mesopotamia the archaeologist can watch the several stages of the revolution at a number of different sites in the south, in Sumer, at Eridu, Ur, Erech, Lagash, Larsa, Shuruppak; the later stages can also be observed in the north, in Akkad, at Kish, Jemdet Nasr, Opis, Eshnunna and Mari. In Sumer at each site the economic systems at the start and at the end are not only similar, but identical; and ultimately this identity proves to be founded on a common language, religion, and social organization. The events revealed by the excavations at Erech may accordingly be taken as illustrating what was happening at other sites.

Erech began as a village of neolithic farmers. The decay and renewal of successive villages, as described on p. 39, gradually formed a mound or *tell* that slowly rose above the level of the marshy plain. The first fifty feet of this artificial hill consist entirely of the ruins of reed huts or mud-brick houses. The simple relics collected from them illustrate the progress summarized in the last chapter—an increasing use of metal, the introduction of the potter's wheel, and so on. The village is growing in size and wealth, but it remains a village.

But then, instead of the walls and hearths of modest huts, appear the foundations of a truly monumental building—a temple or group of temples. And close by rises an artificial mountain, the prototype of the "ziggurat" or staged tower that was an indispensable part of an historical Sumerian temple. This first ziggurat was built entirely of hand-formed lumps of mud with layers of bitumen between them. But it towered more than thirty-five feet above the then existing surface of the ground—the street-level of the contemporary settlement—and its top measured over 1000 yards square. The mountain's steeply-sloping sides were relieved by buttresses alternating with recesses, and were further adorned and consolidated by thousands of little pottery tumblers. These had been pushed side by side in close-packed rows into the mud of the ziggurat while it was still wet. They served to consolidate the faces while they were drying, and eventually stood out forming decorative patterns of round dimples when the monument was complete.

On the mountain-top was a tiny shrine with white-washed walls of mud brick and a staircase by which the deity might descend from the heavens. At the foot were more imposing temples.

The erection of the artificial mountain and of the temples, the collection and transportation of the materials, the manufacture of the thousands of pots and bricks required a large and disciplined force of laborers and craftsmen. While these were withdrawn from food-production they must have been supported, if not paid, from some common store of surplus food. Whose? Presumably it was already controlled by the power, we may perhaps say already "deity," to whose honor and glory the buildings were dedicated. The fertility of the land and the pious superstitions of its cultivators must have endowed its divine lord with riches at least in surplus foodstuffs.

But the erection of such a monument required more than laborers and their food. The whole was carefully planned: the artificial mountain was laid out with its corners to the cardinal points. A centralized directing force was requisite. The god being but a fictitious projection of the communal will, that force must have been supplied by his servants. Naturally enough the imaginary god has found earthly representatives and interpreters glad to administer and to enlarge his terrestrial possessions in exchange for a modest share of his income. The wizards and magicians, guessed at in neolithic villages, have emerged as a corporation of priests sanctified with divine authority and emancipated from any mundane labors in field or pasture. These interpret the divine will to the toiling masses or, in other words, twist the magic ceremonies, by which society would compel natural forces, into ever more complicated rites for conciliating the power that now personifies these. And in this process of invention there are revealed the plans of temples, just as historical kings relate that the plan for a temple has been revealed to them in a dream.

We may assume then that, as in the earliest historical period, a corporation of priests already corresponds to this first of temples. And, as in all written documents, these priests must have provided the administrators of the god's treasury. But the administration of the rich treasures of the temple would impose quite a new task on the persons engaged. What those tasks were, written documents will soon reveal: it may be anticipated that some means had to be devised for keeping track of the various offerings and of their utilization, lest the deity should demand of his priest accounts of his stewardship. And, in fact, in the ziggurat-shrine the excavators found a tablet bearing the impression of a seal and hollows that are certainly numerals. It is the world's oldest account tablet, the immediate forerunner of a long series of Sumerian temple accounts.

Thus the first temple at Erech reveals a community, raised to the dignity of a city, disposing of a surplus of real wealth accumulated in the hands of a deity and administered by a corporation of priests. It implies an organized force of workers, specialized industries and some rudimentary system of commerce and transportation. And at this crucial moment the beginnings at least of accountancy and even writing emerge. And, of course, Erech did not stand alone; the sites of the other great Sumerian cities have yielded remains of the same cultural stage and of a like absolute antiquity. And from this point the development of urban civilization can be traced continuously till the moment when the full light of written history dawns upon it and within it. The story is one of accumulating wealth, of improving technical skill, of increasing specialization of labor, and of expanding trade.

The temple at Erech fell into disrepair, and was rebuilt at least four times. Each successive temple is grander than its predecessor. The pots hammered into the walls of the first ziggurat are replaced by cones of baked clay, the ends of which are painted black, red, and white. These are stuck into the mud-brick walls so as to make mosaic patterns. By the beginning of the historical period inlays of mother-of-pearl and carnelian on black bitumen replace the mosaic of clay cones. The inner walls of the sanctuary are decorated at first with figures of animals molded in clay. Later these are replaced by friezes of plaques cut out of stone or shell and mounted in bitumen. At the dawn of history large-size groups of animals in copper, cast or beaten up over a core of bitumen, replace the molded clay figures.

The stage represented by the third principal phase of rebuilding at Erech is equally well known in Akkad (Northern Babylonia), particularly at Jemdet Nasr. By this time increase of wealth, a profounder knowledge of applied chemistry and geology, and more regular and extended commerce are disclosed by the importation and utilization of lead, silver, and lapis lazuli. Increased technical skill is indicated by the manufacture of articles in glazed paste and of light war-chariots. And now the account tablets are regularly inscribed with symbols and numerals. The symbols are mainly pictures, but include already conventional signs that are hardly recognizable as likenesses of concrete objects, but must already posses a conventional meaning. There are different numeral signs for units, tens, and sixties or hundreds. The tablets already apply simple arithmetical formulas—reckoning, for instance, the area of a field as the product of two adjacent sides.

The growth of the god's revenues, and the consequent increase in the complexity of accountancy, have compelled the priestly administrators to devise systems of writing and numeral notation intelligible to their colleagues and successors in the permanent corporation of temple officers. To simplify and abbreviate their labors they have had to discover and formulate rules of reckoning and "laws" of geometry.

By the next phase, well after 3000 B.C., the "royal cemetery" of Ur brilliantly illustrates the culmination of the process. Goldsmiths can now make wire and solder; they produce delicate chains and elaborate ornaments in granulation and filigree work. The coppersmith is master of the hammer and of casting, and is probably employing the *cire perdue* process. And so he can provide his fellow-craftsmen with a variety of delicate and specialized tools—axes, adzes, chisels, gouges, drills, knives, saws, nails, clamps, needles, and so on. Jewelers can now pierce the hardest stones and engrave them for seals. Sculptors are beginning to carve vases and statuettes out of limestone and even basalt. The carpenter, besides boats, chariots, and couches, fashions harps and lyres. Naturally there are professional musicians to play upon them; these actually take their places in the tomb beside their royal masters.

All this luxury and refinement means more than accumulated wealth and intensified specialization. It reposes on an enriched craft-lore and new discoveries in applied science. The fine castings of the Sumerian smiths could not have been achieved with pure copper. They are hardly conceivable unless the alloy of copper with tin that we term bronze had been discovered, and actual analyses have demonstrated the employment of this alloy. This does not in itself vindicate for the Sumerians the credit of the discovery; bronze was also used in India about the same date. It presumably began as an accidental alloy resulting from smelting a copper ore containing tin as a natural impurity or from chance mixtures of copper and tin ores. But it is only in an urban industry using "copper" drawn from a variety of different sources that comparison would reveal the superiority of the "copper" from one district or ore. That observation must be the first step to the isolation of the impurity to which that superiority was due, and so to the deliberate preparation of the alloy. Bronze can have been discovered only by deliberate comparison and experimentation.

Other evidence of experimentation is afforded by a small

dagger of iron belonging to the same period. It had been made, not from meteoric iron or natural telluric iron, but from metal reduced from its ore. It may have been the result of an isolated experiment, and there is no evidence that the discovery was followed up. It was not till about 1300 B.C. that iron came into regular industrial use, and then not in Mesopotamia, but elsewhere in Asia Minor. Yet another discovery of the period was clear glass. Glazed stones and fayence had been known to the prehistoric Egyptians, and the art of their manufacture had been introduced into Mesopotamia before 3000 B.C. But some time after that date we have examples of clear glass. This may rank as a Sumerian discovery resulting from experiments with the other glazes, all of which depend upon the properties of alkaline silicates.

The employment on such a vast scale of imported substances foreign to the alluvial plains implies that the commercial relations foreshadowed in earlier periods had been extended and made more regular. Some of the copper was brought from Oman south of the Persian Gulf. Silver and lead probably came from the Taurus mountains in Asia Minor, attested as a great exporting center soon after 2500 B.C. Large shells were derived from the Persian Gulf and the Arabian Sea. Timber must have been brought from mountains that catch the rain—from the Zagros, or perhaps even from Lebanon on the Mediterranean coast. Lapis is believed to have been derived from Afghanistan.

And trade did not stop short at raw materials. The second revolution was already being accomplished in Egypt and India; the cities of Sumer were in commercial relations with others on the Nile and the Indus. Commodities manufactured by the specialized industries of one urban center were traded to the bazaars of another. In several Mesopotamian cities stray seals, beads, and even pots have turned up that are not Sumerian in character, but are, on the other hand, common in contemporary cities in Sindh and Punjab. They afford conclusive proof of international trade linking the Tigris with the Indus 1200 miles away. They reveal a picture of caravans regularly crossing the rugged ranges and salt deserts that separate the two valleys, or of fleets of dhows sailing along the waterless coasts of the Arabian Sea between the rivers' mouths.

Now that sort of commerce in the Orient is not, and never can have been, a mere transportation of bales of merchandise from place to place. At the termini and at stations on the way the caravans and merchant dhows must make prolonged halts. Representatives, probably colonists from the exporting country, must receive the goods at their destination and arrange a return load, entertaining the travelers in the meantime. Just as there are permanent colonies of British merchants in Oporto, Stamboul, and Shanghai, so we may imagine colonies of Indian merchants settled at Ur and Kish. Trade under such conditions is very really a means of intercourse, a channel by which ideas can be diffused on an international scale.

Again, it is not only goods—the concrete embodiments of new inventions—but also men—artisans and inventors—that are transported by the caravans. In the Orient skilled labor is surprisingly mobile, and it is so traditionally. Craftsmen gravitate to centers where they can profitably employ their skill. And this must be true of antiquity. The new class of expert craftsmen, created by the second revolution, had been liberated from the tasks of primary food-production, and so from attachment to the soil. They were perhaps at the same time released from tribal bonds and not yet firmly attached to the nascent local States. So they could move whithersoever profitable employment offered. Or, were they slaves, they would be sent as commodities to where their skill would fetch the highest price for their persons. In any case, this mobility explains the rapid diffusion of technical processes.

Such were the stages of the second revolution in Mesopotamia and such its industrial and economic consequences for man's material culture. The several stages are undoubtedly moments in an organic process of economic accumulation and of scientific and technical advancement. But this continuity need not apply to the ethnological and political domains. There are, indeed, indications that accumulation and advancement were interrupted or promoted by the advent of new peoples, perhaps by conquests and invasions.

So, for instance, burial rites were changed. The neolithic farmers were generally buried extended, lying full length upon their backs. In the cultural phase III (represented at Jemdet Nasr) the dead were interred crouched with the knees drawn up to the chin; in the royal cemetery of Ur the skeletons generally lie flexed in the attitude of sleep, while some personages, supposedly royalties, are laid to rest in monumental tombs surrounded with human victims, sacrificed at their obsequies. Some changes in architecture too seem to indicate more than mere technical advances. The second temple-complex at Erech rests on foundations of limestone blocks, a material that seems exotic in the alluvial plain. In the next group stone is abandoned and flat kiln-fired bricks are used. But the last group of temples and all contemporary monuments are built of absurd plano-convex bricks, flat on one face only, but cushion-shaped on the other. It has been thought that the new architectural devices represent foreign fashions introduced into Sumer by invaders from abroad. Sealings certainly give indications of warfare and battles. And at the end, when written records become explicit, we find Babylonia occupied by two distinct linguistic groups: some of its inhabitants speak Sumerian, others talk a Semitic dialect— Akkadian—allied to Hebrew and Arabic, but radically different from Sumerian.

The nature and effects of the rather problematical ethnic and racial disturbances cannot be defined precisely. They certainly did not seriously interrupt the continuity of material culture. And the gods and their temples survived the crises; the priestly corporations retained their identity whatever happened to other social structures. And that was true of all subsequent history. The written records of Babylonia describe frequent chances of dynasty and frequent conquests by foreign invaders. In these catastrophes temples might be plundered and wrecked, but the new king or the successful conqueror regularly displayed his piety and his power by rebuilding and enriching with fresh revenues the city temples. As late as 323 B.C. Alexander of Macedon sealed his conquest of Asia by rebuilding the E-sagile, the great temple of Babylon. The repeated reconstruction of the prehistoric temples at Erech and the other cities is concrete testimony to the same continuity of religious corporations with their unbroken cultural traditions that history unambiguously attests later on.

Now, as the temple corporations, continuing through all vicissitudes, grew richer, the task of administering the growing revenues became heavier and heavier. The administrators had to devise ever better means for recording their complicated business transactions. Eventually they created a system of writing which not only their colleagues and immediate successors, but also modern scholars could read. By the period of the fourth temple complex at Erech decipherable written documents emerge to supplement the deductions of prehistoric archaeology.

Soon after 3000 B.C. the earliest written texts give us a picture of the social and economic organization of Sumer and Akkad. The land is divided up among fifteen or twenty city States, each politically autonomous, but all enjoying a common material culture, a common religion, and a common language, and all largely interdependent economically. The center of each city was the sacred *temenos* or citadel containing the temples of the city god and other deities. We may, if we like, infer that the god is a personification of magic forces; dramatic representations of the death and rebirth of

vegetation, of sowing and harvest, may once have been performed as magic rites designed to compel the germination of
the crops. In time the actors who symbolized the grain and its
magic fertility would be taken as playing the role of a deity
who controlled the magic forces. The magic force which man
had sought to compel would be personified as a god who
must be helped and conciliated. Before history begins, society
has projected its collective will, its corporate hopes and fears,
into this fictitious person whom it reveres as Lord of its
territory.

In any case, each god has an earthly dwelling, the city
temple, a material estate, and human servants, the priestly
corporation. The oldest decipherable documents from Mesopotamia are, in fact, the accounts of the temple revenues kept
by the priests. They reveal the temple as not only the center
of the city's religious life, but also the nucleus of capital
accumulation. The temple functions as the great bank; the
god is the chief capitalist of the land. The early temple archives
record the god's loans of seed or plow animals to cultivators,
the fields he has let to tenants, wages paid to brewers, boat-
builders, spinners, and other employees, advances of grain or
bullion to traveling merchants. The god is the richest member
of the community. His wealth is available to the community
from whose piety he, in fact, derived it. But the same piety
required that the borrower should not only pay back the loan,
but also add a little thank-offering. The god's ministers were
doubtless careful to remind you of your duty, and even
stipulated in advance what decency demanded you to offer.
Such thank-offerings would today be called interest, and the
temple's tariff might be styled usurious by the impious.

This economic system that made the god a great capitalist
and landlord, his temple into a city bank, evidently goes back
to remote prehistoric times. The figured gypsum tablet from
the oldest temple at Erech, the tablets from Jemdet Nasr
with their picture-writing, are undoubtedly precursors of the
temple accounts that can now be read. The latter accordingly
justify the description of Sumer's economic development already deduced. They will form the basis of the analysis of the
second revolution's scientific consequences to be given in the
next chapter.

But by 3000 B.C. there is already emerging beside the deity
in every city a temporal potentate. He styles himself humbly
the god's "vicegerent," but also boldly "king." Perhaps he had
once impersonated the god in those sacred dramas imagined
above as a factor in the genesis of godhead. Indeed, he still
takes the part of the god in some acts of the drama. But he

has emancipated himself from the fate of the original actor—
to be consigned to the tomb as the seed is to the earth. And
he has certainly usurped a substantial share of the god's temporal power over men. He even oppresses his subjects according to quite early documents. The State has, indeed, "arisen
out of Society, places itself above it, and separates itself from
it."

Nevertheless, the king fulfilled essential economic functions in the development of Sumerian society. He was possessed of the material power of a civil ruler and a military
commander. One use of this power may have been to see
that "the antagonisms," generated by the revolution, "classes
with conflicting interests, did not consume themselves and
society in sterile struggle." But of that the records are silent.
They do mention the use of the State's power to supplement
the work of "private enterprise" in providing for the economic
needs of the country. Early kings boast of their economic
activities—of cutting canals, of building temples, of importing
timber from Syria, and copper and granite from Oman. They
are sometimes depicted on monuments in the garb of brick-
layers or masons and of architects receiving the plan of a
temple from its god.

Doubtless the royal power accelerated the accumulation of
capital in foodstuffs and real wealth. Courtiers, ministers,
musicians, and men-at-arms were supported by the surplus
thus extorted. And the army was fulfilling an economic function in guarding the city, its canals, its irrigated fields and
pastures against the incursions of starveling nomads from
the surrounding steppes or wild tribes from the mountains. In
the end it would create a political order more compatible with
economic realities than the system of city-states.

Lower Mesopotamia is a geographical unit, dependent for
life on the waters of its twin rivers, for a civilized life on the
importation of the same exotic substances from common
sources. Precisely because they were dependent on the waters
of the same rivers, disputes about lands and water rights were
liable to arise between the several autonomous cities. Just because all relied on the same foreign trade to bring them the
same necessities for industry, commercial rivalries were inevitable amongst sovereign states; the contradiction between an
economic system that ought to be unitary and political sepa-
ratism was made manifest in interminable dynastic wars. Our
earliest documents after the temple accounts, in fact, record
wars between adjacent cities and treaties that temporarily
ended them. The ambition of any city dynast was to obtain
hegemony over his neighbors.

But no permanent result was obtained by these internecine conflicts till 2500 (or later) B.C. Then the Semitic ruler or Agade or Akkad whom we term Sargon established an empire over all Babylonia which lasted with intervals of revolt for nearly a century. His feat was subsequently imitated, more or less successfully, by kings of Ur and of other cities. But only a little after (or before) 1800 B.C. was Babylonia made a political reality, a unified nation with a common capital, a common code of written law, a common calendar, and a permanent system of government by Hammurabi, king of Babylon. Then at last the city-state was absorbed into the territorial state that corresponded on the whole to the realities of economic needs.

In Egypt it seems as if political unification coincided with the accomplishment of the second economic revolution. The Nile Valley is geographically even more a natural economic unit than is the plain of the Tigris and Euphrates, and so the natural factors tending to unity were more efficient. At the same time, the contrast between the narrow valley of Upper Egypt and the open Delta, Lower Egypt, is fundamental. Historically the unification of Egypt means the union of these Two Lands in a single kingdom. That event preceded Sargon's unification of Babylonia by some five centuries, so that the second revolution in the two regions is approximately contemporary.

Egypt is again less completely dependent on imports from abroad than is Mesopotamia. In particular, local supplies of excellent flint rendered metal less essential for industrial purposes; indeed, stone was still being used by Egyptian farmers and artisans a thousand years after their Babylonian contemporaries had been using only metal tools. It was, in fact, primarily luxury articles and magic necessities—malachite, gems, gold, spices—that had to be imported into Egypt. It was accordingly only a demand for such substances on a large scale that made inevitable the systematic organization of external trade and the specialization of manufacturing industries. That demand became effective only through the rise of a class that set an extravagant value on the exotic materials for magical purposes, and at the same time disposed of the surplus wealth needed to gratify their desires.

And so the reserves of supplies required for the transformation of the economic system were not accumulated in the temples of a communal deity, but in the hands of a monarch who had already placed himself above the society from which he had arisen. The unification of Egypt and creation of a state based on secondary industry and commerce as well as food-production were finally accomplished when a king of Upper Egypt, Menes, conquered the Delta. His ancestors have left no concrete memorials of their rise to power comparable to the prehistoric temples of Sumer. And so we have to reconstruct the course of the revolution, the rise of the monarchy, by hazardous inferences from later literary sources, instead of reading off the concrete record of archaeological remains.

A plausible but rather speculative, and certainly much oversimplified, account of the genesis of the Egyptian monarchy would run as follows. In the prehistoric village, communities of self-sufficing food-producing clans whose cemeteries line the Nile Valley may have fallen under the sway of a class of magicians. By the time most individual villagers, having found their private magics futile, were prepared to rely on the magic of the cleverer persons, some acquired a little authority by successful pretensions to influence the fertility of the crops, the weather, and the Nile flood. The invention of a calendar making possible the accurate prediction of the flood's advent would, as suggested on p. 111, be a sure way of justifying such pretensions and consolidating such authority. To enforce them the actual power of cutting off real water by blocking irrigation channels would be an effective means.

But it is likely that our hypothetical magician-chiefs would have enjoyed only a limited tenure of authority, as did the historical chiefs who ruled Nilotic tribes last century. Their magic powers would be regarded as correlative to physical powers. Only a healthy and vigorous chief would perform efficiently the requisite rites; before old age impaired his potency he must be slain to make room for a young and virile successor.

That fate might be escaped could a chief persuade his followers that by his secret magic he could secure immunity from physical infirmities. One of Menes' ancestors may, in fact, have established some such claim to magic rejuvenation. In any case, all historical pharaohs performed periodically a rite—the Sed-festival—that seems designed to secure a renewal of youth by a simulated death and resurrection. By this rite, modeled on the agricultural festivals mentioned on p. 123, 124, pharaoh rose after his symbolic death magically restored to youth, like the grain that has been sown.

Perhaps at the same time the magic chief contrived to identify himself with the totem of his clan and to monopolize communion with the animal or object that all clansmen had once revered as their common ancestor. In any case, Menes and his successors are identified with the Falcon, Horus, who had been just the totem of his clan. But, as we saw on p. 84, there had been other totems belonging to other clans. The unification of Egypt was the victory of Horus, now personified in the chief of the Falcon clan, over all other totems; the latter were degraded to the rank of second-class gods or local deities.

Now the Egyptians had always entertained particularly vivid ideas about the continuance of existence after death. In prehistoric times they behaved as if they believed that the dead man in his grave wanted the food, vessels, and ornaments he had enjoyed or used in real life. . . . In historical times they behaved as if their king's body from the tomb could still secure for them the magic benefits he had conferred upon them in his life. And the king for his part behaved as if after death he could by magic means ensure to himself enjoyment of the substantial pleasures enjoyed upon earth.

The Egyptian monarchy owed its power, on the one hand, to material victories—the overthrow of rival chiefs and king-lets—of which the conquest of the Delta was the last; but, on the other hand, it owed its authority to the rather contradictory ideas of the king's immortality that have just been described. Conquest made Menes master of stupendous resources—the booty from his conquests and thereafter the permanent revenue from the land of which he was theoretically the absolute owner and practically the feudal overlord. But this concentrated wealth was employed primarily in safeguarding that immortality which guaranteed it.

Of course, kings really died and were succeeded by sons or brothers. There were even changes of dynasty in circumstances that elude us. But the idea of the divine king, a hierarchy of officials appointed by the king, and the State organization that he created and they administered constituted effective elements of continuity. Throughout the Old Kingdom the pharaoh's authority as god, his magic power to guarantee the land's prosperity, was being continually cemented by the invention of new rites and the accretion of new attributes. With the rise of Dynasty III and the transfer of the capital from Abydos in Upper Egypt to Memphis near the Delta's apex, the king begins to absorb the life-giving qualities of the Sun, the power that, with the Nile, must have appeared to the Egyptians the source of fertility and wealth. By the Vth Dynasty pharaoh has become Son of the Sun, consubstantial with that beneficent power.

Yet, of course, the divine pharaoh did not earn obedience by conferring on his subjects only fictitious blessings. His authority was consolidated by tangible economic benefits conferred upon his kingdom. Like the unsubstantial deities of

Mesopotamia, this substantial god devoted part of his power and wealth to the material prosperity of his kingdom; a share of his revenues was invested in genuinely reproductive undertakings. A pharaoh of Dynasty II is represented "cutting the first sod" of a new irrigation canal. Operations instituted by the king for the control of the floodwaters are mentioned. From the foundation of the unified kingdom under Menes a special gauge, the Nilometer, was constructed to measure the height of the Nile, and records were kept of the floods. These measurements and records were designed primarily to serve as a basis for the assessment of taxes. But, like the calendar, they indirectly helped the farmer as well as the tax-gatherer.

The importation of raw materials, needed for the development of Egyptian industries as well as for funerary ceremonies, was financed from the royal revenues. Copper and turquoise were mined in Sinai. Expeditions, equipped by the State and escorted by royal soldiers, were periodically dispatched across the desert for the purpose. It was the same with the importation of cedar wood and resins from North Syria. Ships for the voyage to Byblos were equipped and provided with trade goods by the State. Similarly, government officials led expeditions to the Upper Nile and brought back gold and spices.

The principal object of this foreign trade was doubtless to secure luxuries and magic substances or war materials— while peasants and laborers still used stone tools in the fields and quarries, soldiers were armed with metal weapons. Still, commerce brought materials essential to progress in civilization and in science. It offered a livelihood for new classes— merchants, sailors, porters, soldiers, artisans, and clerks— supported from the surplus revenues collected by the pharaoh.

Finally, the monarchy from its foundation conferred upon the Egyptians real benefits that the Sumerians still lacked. A series of villages strung out along the banks of a single river are liable to be involved in mutual squabbles over boundaries and water rights. Actually throughout Egyptian history right down to modern times such parochial disputes have broken out violently whenever the central government is weak. Menes and his successors repressed such wasteful conflicts as long as the Old Kingdom endured. And besides maintaining internal peace, they preserved the land from foreign aggression. The arid plateaus on either side of the Nile Valley were sparsely populated by tribes of poor pastoralists and hunters. Such were liable at any moment to raid the fertile valley. The Delta was exposed to attack from Libyans on the west and from bedouins on the east. Nubians, perhaps still in the stage of nomadic garden-culture, were constantly pressing downstream into Upper Egypt. The army, which had been the instrument of forcible unification, was employed thereafter to ward off such plunderers and trespassers. Quite early texts disclose the organization of a regular system of defense through the establishment of frontier posts manned by permanent garrisons commanding the ways of access to the Nile Valley.

It was, of course, these realist measures that promoted the extraordinary growth in wealth and population reflected in the archaeological record after Menes' conquest. But it has been necessary to explain the peculiar ideology associated with those measures, because in the archaeological record economic achievements and scientific discoveries appear only as applied to magical ends, as distorted in an ideological medium.

Down to 2000 B.C. the archaeological record of Egypt consists almost entirely of graves and their furniture. From perhaps 5000 to about 3000 B.C. extend pre-dynastic cemeteries of simple pit-graves furnished more or less richly with home-made articles (p. 127 above). Modest improvements in tomb construction, the appearance of imported luxuries in growing numbers, occasional copper implements and beads of fayence illustrate the advances and discoveries described in Chapter VI. The unification of Egypt under Menes and his immediate successors (Dynasty I) is symbolized by the construction near Abydos of monumental tombs which find only remote and vague precursors among the later pre-dynastic graves.

The royal tombs of Abydos were miniature palaces of brick and timber erected at the bottom of vast pits dug in the desert sand. There are also mastabas of mud brick built above ground to serve as funeral shrines for the cult of the dead and storehouses for mortuary offerings. The tombs are furnished with a quite unprecedented wealth and variety of exquisitely wrought furniture, weapons, vessels, toilet articles, and ornaments wrought with masterly perfection of cedar-wood, gold, copper, alabaster, obsidian, lapis lazuli, turquoise, and other choice materials, native or foreign. The storerooms are crowded with well-made pots containing oil, beer, grain, and other foodstuffs. Inscriptions on seals and wooden tablets, recording outstanding events of the reign, prove that a system of writing had already been invented, although the script is still primitive. Servants and officials are buried in rooms adjacent to the royal burial chamber, and have presumably been slain to accompany their master.

A multitude of laborers must have been employed in digging the grave-shafts, in preparing and transporting the bricks and planks, and in erecting the tombs and mastabas. The subtly

fashioned articles deposited therein are indubitably the products of specialized and highly trained carpenters, smiths, stonecutters, engravers, goldsmiths, and jewelers. These laborers
and expert artisans, withdrawn from primary production, have
been paid by the surplus collected by the monarch—the booty
of conquest and the tribute regularly exacted. And that surplus
must have been used for securing the foreign materials, like
cedar-wood, copper, obsidian, and lapis lazuli, so lavishly employed. Inscriptions in the tombs attest already the existence
of scribes and officials charged with the collection and administration of the royal revenues, the planning and direction
of building operations, and other functions. The unification of
Egypt has, in fact, evoked the same new classes and the same
new professions as the urban revolution in Sumer. But their
services seem to be devoted primarily to the conservation of
royal corpses.

To the same end were applied the growing resources, the
fresh scientific discoveries of subsequent reigns. To secure
greater permanence and security for the king's last resting-
place, the tomb came to be hewn out of the living rock under
Dynasty III. The quarrymen thus learned to carve the hardest
rocks with rudimentary tools; the architects had to plan and
lay out a complex of galleries and shafts that they could never
look at as a whole (they had, that is, to solve the same problems as are involved in drilling a tunnel or a mine gallery).
Corbelled vaults of mud brick were employed even under
Dynasty II; by Dynasty III the principle of the true arch (with
keystone) had been mastered and applied.

The overground monuments—mastabas and funerary
chapels—were similarly elaborated. Under Dynasty III stone
replaced mud brick to give the structure greater permanence.
The bundles of papyrus reeds that had once supported the
king's earthly palace were thus converted into fluted columns
of imperishable stone—an idea which we have inherited
through Greece from IIIrd Dynasty Egypt. The colored reed
mats that once hung between the papyrus columns were
copied in glazed tiles under Zoser. Under the same monarch,
the mastaba, now built of stone, was enlarged, becoming the
so-called stepped pyramid. Cheops in Dynasty IV then translated this into the true pyramid.

The execution of such works required a gigantic labor force.
The huge blocks of limestone or granite for the pyramid,
weighing anything up to 350 tons, were quarried at Tura, on
the east bank of the Nile, floated downstream to Gizah above
Cairo, and then dragged up a ramp to the level of the plateau
100 feet above the river. Herodotus was told that 100,000

men were employed continually for ten years on quarrying the stone alone. Though not "free workers," the army of quarrymen, masons, and porters were provided with food and shelter out of the royal revenues. Though many must have perished, it is still likely that this distribution of wealth promoted a growth in population.

But not only labor was required: the architects had to learn to co-ordinate and control this vast force of workers and to solve the mechanical problems of applying manpower to the lifting of heavy and unwieldy blocks. Moreover, a mystical significance seems to have attached to the accuracy of the structure's orientation and proportion. The success achieved is surprising. The base of the great pyramid is intended to be a perfect square, with a side of 775¾ feet. The error, according to modern measurements, does not exceed one inch in any side!

The accuracy of Egyptian workmanship was largely achieved by inexhaustible patience and trial-and-error. But a monument like a pyramid must have been planned to scale in advance and precisely measured. Its execution is hardly conceivable without prior calculations involving geometrical formulas. Extant mathematical texts confirm this expectation. For example, they contain a whole group of problems devoted to calculating the batter of a pyramid. The sepulchral monuments, indeed, imply the application of a considerable body of mathematical knowledge. The Egyptians' peculiar beliefs about dead kings seem thus to have inspired scientific discoveries that had more practical uses too.

By the IVth Dynasty care for the conservation of the body had led to the development of mummification, giving employment to a whole class of professional embalmers and affording exceptional opportunities for the accumulation of knowledge of human anatomy. In the pre-dynastic graves contact with the dry desert sand had sufficed to preserve the flesh and hair of corpses. Enclosed in coffins of wood or alabaster and in built tombs after the revolution, the bodies were no longer naturally preserved from putrescence. To stay its ravages chemical methods of embalming and a ritual of magic spells were gradually elaborated.

The deceased's survival could further be ensured by carving likenesses in wood or stone—portrait statues of him. These had to be "animated" by magical means. And to be effective they must be as lifelike as possible. Hence the superb naturalism of some Old Kingdom statues and bas reliefs.

The dead man needed in the afterworld the objects and the services he enjoyed here. Hence not only were the tombs liber-

ally provided with furniture and offerings, but estates were
set apart to provide a permanent supply of the requisite offerings to the deceased. To ensure his enjoyment of this provision,
magic pictures of the life of the estate were painted on the
tomb walls, already under Dynasty IV and more regularly
later. These pictures are our best source for the secular life
and economic organization of Egypt in the later days of the
Old Kingdom. They depict an economic unit that is not a city,
but a large farm like a medieval manor. The farm is worked
by peasants under the administration of bailiffs or overseers.
The scenes include the work in the field, the breeding of cattle,
hunting and fishing. And we see the peasants coming in to pay

FIG. 8.—GOLDSMITH'S WORKSHOP FROM AN OLD KINGDOM
TOMB PAINTING.

their rent or dues, always in kind, while a scribe notes down
on papyrus what each man brings and an overseer with a whip
keeps the tributaries up to the mark. But the estate was not
purely agricultural; it included potteries, smithies, carpenters'
and jewelers' workshops. Here again we see overseers weighing out quantities of material to the craftsmen and scribes noting down the amounts issued.

The manorial community looks very like a self-sufficing
unit with specialized labor and graded classes. It is, of course,
in reality inconceivable apart from the larger economic system
that is the Egyptian State. That system provides the manor's
artisans with their raw materials, and absorbs the surplus
products of the farm. And we know that genuine cities existed
even though none has so far been excavated from this period.

With the political unification of Egypt there emerged in the
Nile Valley an economic system in which manufacture and
commerce ranked on a par with the production of foodstuffs
by farming, hunting, and fishing. This revolution in Egypt had

the same effect on population as in the cities of Mesopotamia. And, as there, it coincided with the first development of writing and mathematics. Nevertheless, now that we have examined them at close quarters, the two systems appear remarkably dissimilar. The contrast is no longer confined to the individual products of the several trades, but affects even fundamentals: the focus of accumulation appears in the one area a priestly corporation, in the other an individual monarch; the economic unit in Sumer is a city with outlying fields and hamlets which could and did function by itself. In Egypt, on the contrary, the unit is the kingdom as a royal estate; the manors or cities into which it may be subdivided would cease to function if isolated from it, or rather would relapse into more or less self-sufficing peasant communities. Egyptian civilization is in no sense a colonial outpost of the Sumerian nor vice versa.

The same contrasts, overshadowing all abstract agreements, would probably be revealed did written documents supplement the archaeological record in the Indus valley. There the second revolution had been probably contemporary with that in Egypt and Sumer, and was in any case perfected by 2500 B.C. By that date large cities had been established in Sindh and the Punjab. They may exceed a square mile in area. The houses are built mainly of kiln-fired bricks, and boast at least two stories. The streets and alleys on which they open have evidently been laid out in conformity with a preconceived plan which is preserved through several periods of reconstruction. A system of sewers serves the houses. Among these can be distinguished shops and factories, the sumptuous abodes of wealthy merchants or officials, and the hovels of artisans and transport workers.

The buildings and articles found in them have been produced by specialized craftsmen—brickmakers, carpenters, potters, coppersmiths, glaziers, stonecutters, goldsmiths, and jewelers. The regularity of the streets implies a civic authority with officials to enforce its decisions. Public servants were required for cleaning the drains. There must have been a class of clerks, since a system of writing and numeral notation was in use as well as standardized weights and measures.

All these classes, evidently very numerous, must be supported by the surplus foodstuffs produced by peasants living in the city or in suburban villages. But even fishermen, toiling far away on the Arabian Sea, made contributions; for dried sea-fish was imported. The urban artisans, for their part, must produce a surplus of manufactured commodities to be bartered for the raw materials needed in industry, but un-

obtainable on the alluvial plain. Not only have the cities of
the plain yielded deodara wood, imported from the Himalayas,
and metals and precious stones brought from distant highlands, but commodities manufactured in the cities have been
found in prehistoric villages among the hills of Baluchistan
and even far away in Mesopotamia.

The prehistory of the Indus civilization is still unknown;
the simpler villages and townships from which the cities have
arisen remain unidentified. By 2500 B.C. the same uniform
civilization extends from the mouth of the Indus throughout
the lowlands of the Punjab right up to the foothills, but there
is no evidence whether any political unity corresponded to this
cultural uniformity. It is even uncertain what was the nucleus
of capital accumulation. We have indications of a division
into classes of rich and poor, but whether a king or a god
stood at the head of the hierarchy is uncertain. Both temples
and palaces are so inconspicuous among the ruins that their
very existence is dubious.

The revolutions just described occurred almost simultaneously in Egypt and Sumer, and probably in India too. In each
case the revolution was based on the same scientific discoveries, and resulted in the addition to the population of the
same new classes. It is hard to believe in the independence of
these events, especially when the proofs of long-standing intercourse between the areas be recalled. And this intercourse
became closer than ever at the moment of the revolution or
just after it. Just about the time of Egypt's unification, devices
that may reasonably be regarded as Mesopotamian in origin
—cylinder seals, certain artistic motives, crenelated brick
architecture, a new type of boat—appear on the Nile for the
first time. Soon after the revolution Indian manufactures were
being imported into Sumer.

Some sort of diffusion had evidently been going on. Yet
no theory of one-sided dependence is compatible with the
contrasts revealed by closer scrutiny. Urban civilization was
not simply transplanted from one center to another, but was
in each an organic growth rooted in the local soil. If we want
a modern analogy, the establishment of mechanized industry
and factory production by European capitalists in Africa or
India will not serve. We must think rather of the rise of that
system of production in the countries on both sides of the
Atlantic. America, Britain, France, the Low Countries shared
a common scientific, cultural, and mercantile tradition long
before the Industrial Revolution. Despite wars and customs
barriers, the interchange of goods, ideas, and persons went on
continuously. England, indeed, was in the van of the Revolu-

tion itself, but the other countries did not merely copy her
mechanical inventions or economic organization; they had
been experimenting along the same lines, and made independent contributions when the time came. The establishment in China or even Russia of factories and railways
modeled on Western lines and staffed with European and
American managers and technicians was quite a different
process.

And so Egypt, Sumer, and India had not been isolated or
independent before the revolution. All shared more or less a
common cultural tradition to which each had been contributing. And it had been maintained and enriched by a continuous
intercourse involving an interchange of goods, ideas, and
craftsmen. That is the explanation of the observed parallelism.

But once the new economy had been established in the
three primary centers, it spread thence to secondary centers,
much like Western capitalism spread to colonies and economic
dependencies. First on the borders of Egypt, Babylonia, and
the Indus valley—in Crete and the Greek Islands, Syria,
Assyria, Iran, and Baluchistan—then further afield, on the
Greek mainland, the Anatolian plateau, South Russia, we see
villages converted into cities and self-sufficing food-producers
turning to industrial specialization and external trade. And the
process is repeated in ever-widening circles around each secondary and tertiary center.

In the new cities not only abstract agreements in economic
structure and underlying science, but also identity in the forms
of artificial products, like amulets, seals, and letters, demonstrate how many of the vital elements of civilization had been
borrowed from the primary centers on the Nile, the Euphrates,
and the Indus. The second revolution was obviously propagated by diffusion; the urban economy in the secondary centers
was inspired or imposed by the primary foci. And it is easy to
show that the process was inevitable.

The civilizations of the alluvial plains were dependent on the
importation from abroad of raw materials; part of their surplus wealth had to be expended upon obtaining the requisite
imports. But the coveted materials seldom lay in an unin-
habited wilderness. And so communities within whose territories the materials lay could claim a share in the surplus. They
must, indeed, be persuaded to produce more of their metal,
timber, spices, or precious stones than was required for domestic consumption to barter to Egyptians, Sumerians, and
Indians, or at least to lend their services to the latter as guides,
porters, and laborers.

New opportunities of livelihood were thus opened up to the

possessors of industrial materials. But to profit by these opportunities industrial specialization was necessary. The surplus
wealth of the alluvial plain was available to support families in-
habiting metalliferous mountains if those families were withdrawn from food production to mine and transport ore. In
practice, of course, local food production was not arrested, but
the new wealth was employed to support a new population that
on the old economy would have been superfluous and condemned to starvation or emigration. The new role of purveyor
of raw material meant both an increase in population and also
class-divisions. A couple of examples will illustrate the process.

The Egyptians required large quantities of cedar-wood for
tombs, for boat-building, and for furniture. They obtained it
from Lebanon in North Syria, and shipped it from the port of
Byblos (close to Beirut). But long before the rise of the
Egyptian dynasties, Byblos, like other Syrian harbors, was the
site of a township. Its inhabitants, the Giblites of the Bible,
were presumably more or less self-sufficing fishers and farmers.
They had participated in the intercourse outlined in Chapter
VI, and had been in contact with Egypt, and probably with
Mesopotamia too, before the second revolution.

The effect of the revolution in Egypt had been to make effective a tremendous demand for the raw materials Byblos
could supply. In satisfying it, the Giblites had an opportunity
to share in the surplus wealth of Egypt; its expenditure opened
up means of livelihood to families for whom the local farming
and fishing could offer no sustenance. But its acceptance spelt
the final abandonment of economic self-sufficiency. Byblos
would henceforth owe its prosperity to producing for a foreign
market.

Imported articles of Egyptian manufacture, found at Byblos
and going back to the period immediately before Menes' unification, illustrate the Giblites' share in Egypt's prosperity.
And, of course, Egyptian merchants or officials had to settle
there to look after the vital trade, just as English merchant
houses have their representatives in Oporto. The Egyptians in-
structed the Giblites in the administration of the growing city
and the management of their revenues; they may even have
established a sort of protectorate. A stone temple was erected
in the city and was decorated by immigrant Egyptian craftsmen. To meet the needs of commerce the Giblites learned the
Egyptian script.

Thus the Giblites adopted discoveries of the Egyptians, as-
similated their economy to the standards of the urban revolution and increased in numbers. Their township became a city,
and was soon rich enough to become a market for raw mate-

rials from other regions, a secondary center for the diffusion of the new economy. But Giblite civilization was not just a transplantation of the Egyptian; native traditions in architecture, pottery, and other crafts, in dress and religion were conserved. It was the refinements superadded that were taken over from Egypt. And inspiration may have come from other quarters too. On the other hand, Giblite civilization remained provincial as compared with the Egyptian. The borrowed refinements were not developed as they were in the home country. The Egyptians, for instance, improved their script with the passage of time; the Giblites preserved the archaic characters adopted under the early dynasties and kept them unchanged for nearly a thousand years.

In much the same way, the importation of copper, silver, and lead from the Taurus mountains into Mesopotamia resulted in the growth of an urban civilization in Cappadocia on the plateau of Asia Minor. Before 2500 B.C. the native settlements there had scarcely advanced beyond a neolithic economy. The local villagers or townspeople were content with the stone tools and handmade pots produced by unspecialized domestic industry. Soon after 2500 B.C. we read of Assyrian merchants settled among the native townships and trading in ore. A few centuries later the correspondence of such merchants shows how they were bartering Babylonian manufactures for metal and local products. Evidently the surplus wealth of Mesopotamia was providing for miners and smelters who made no direct contribution to the communal food supplies. At the same time, excavation reveals the townships growing into cities dependent on industry and trade. Metal becomes common, pots are manufactured on the wheel by professionals instead of being built up by the housewife. Mesopotamian devices are borrowed to meet the requirements of the new economic situation. The cylinder seal is adopted as a means for labeling property and signing documents. Soon the Babylonian script is adapted to transcribe the local languages. But Cappadocian civilization, like the Giblite, preserved its local peculiarities. And again the borrowed elements were developed more slowly than in Mesopotamia. The local seals, for instance, go on repeating designs a thousand years after they had gone out of fashion in Babylonia.

But often the second revolution was propagated by violence and imposed by the force of imperialism. Some communities were too backward and unenterprising to appreciate the advantages of the new economy and its products. The nomads who hunted or grazed their flocks on the flanks of Sinai were not to be enticed by corn or manufactured trinkets into mining copper for the Egyptians. The mines were exploited by workers sent from Egypt, and the royal army had to protect them against the nomads. From the IInd Dynasty pharaohs have had themselves depicted on the rocks of Sinai "smiting the wretched bedouin." In this case armed intervention did not extend civilization or create new urban centers.

In other cases, however, the victims of imperialism were educated thereby to compete with the aggressors in material culture. The Sumerians had to import their raw materials from lands inhabited by progressive communities like the Elamites, and to reach them the caravans had to traverse similar territories. Now the communities thereby affected often inhabited adequately watered territories and had prospered under a neolithic régime. They did, indeed, adopt devices like the wheeled car and the potters' wheels and imported gold, lapis lazuli, and other luxury articles.

But on the whole they were satisfied with homemade products and could live in modest comfort on their own resources. Their demands for luxury articles were too feeble to persuade them to produce timber or metal in the vast quantities required by the Sumerian cities, or to tolerate caravans disturbing their fields and pastures. They may ultimately have resisted the overtures of Sumerian merchants and attacked their caravans. And then the Sumerians would have to undertake punitive expeditions to secure raw material and to protect trade routes.

Very early texts refer to wars waged by the cities of Sumer and Akkad against Elamites and other "barbarian" neighbors. While these references may refer to raids by impoverished mountaineers upon the rich plains, they may equally indicate struggles of the sort just envisaged. Besides unifying Babylonia, Sargon of Agade embarked upon campaigns of conquest in surrounding regions, the economic motives of which are clear enough. His own inscriptions mention explicitly as objectives the Silver Mountains (Taurus) and the Cedar Forests (? Lebanon). A later document describes how he was invited to Cappadocia to support the metal traders settled there, and refers also to a mountain of lapis lazuli. A still later tablet is to claim a "Tinland" among Sargon's conquest. Undoubtedly he subdued the metalliferous district of Elam and extended his dominions from the Upper Sea (Mediterranean or Caspian) to the Lower Sea (the Persian Gulf), thus embracing the regions on which Babylonia was dependent.

In some instances at least the conquests resulted in the forcible implantation of urban civilization, converting more or less self-sufficing townships into industrial and commercial cities. At Nineveh in Assyria (opposite Mosul), Sargon's

grandson founded a temple to Ishtar, the first of a long series
of temples erected on the site. Now that symbolized an economic revolution; for, as in Sumer, the temple constituted a
permanent center for the accumulation of wealth and the development of industry. Its erection and adornment involved
the expenditure of a surplus that would nourish a prolific, if
servile, proletariat. It would create a new demand for lapis
lazuli, timber, metal, and so on, thus turning Nineveh into a
secondary center of diffusion. This process may have been repeated under Sargon or a little earlier in other Assyrian towns.
And about the same period the Babylonian script and other
devices were introduced, fully formed, into Assyria.

Sargon and his successors can therefore claim to have been
"founders of cities" even where townships had existed long
before them. There is this much truth in the biblical phrase
about "Asshur going forth from Shinar (Sumer) and building
Nineveh," etc. The people of Assyria had not come from
Babylonia, but the earliest temples in what were to be the historical cities of Assyria were founded by Akkadians (Nineveh)
or Sumerians, or were at least furnished with cult statues of
Sumerian type (Assur).

Now Syria and Assyria were certainly populous long before
3000 B.C., very likely even before Sumer was colonized. But
those steppe countries enjoy a regular rainfall, so that the incentive to close social organization that worked so efficaciously
in Lower Mesopotamia was lacking. The population was scattered among numerous permanent villages which grew into
little townships like the modern Kurdish villages. Their prosperous inhabitants had adopted the wheel and other devices,
and occasionally made use of imported substances like lapis
lazuli, gold, and copper. But at least down to 3000 B.C. they
preserved their economic independence; they remained content with stone tools and weapons, and so did not have to rely
on imports. But after 3000 B.C.—perhaps, indeed, as late as
the time of Sargon—they suddenly began to use metal regularly. Their tools and weapons are all of distinctively Sumerian
form, so that there is no doubt who were their instructors in
metallurgy. And the sacrifice of self-sufficiency thus attested
was accompanied by other familiar signs of the second revolution; soon some towns begin to expand into cities, while a few
are absorbed by more successful neighbors. It is by no means
certain how far the revolution here was the result of actual
conquest by Sargon or by some Sumerian precursor. Even the
cities that may most plausibly be claimed as Akkadian foundations did not remain colonies and dependencies for long.
They had never lost their native culture, and soon became

centers of revolt, and ultimately at times the capitals of new States like Assur itself.

For economic imperialism did not propagate the second revolution only by conquest. Successful resistance to its attacks or the threat thereof was only possible by assimilating part of the civilization of the aggressors. Stone weapons were no more a match for the bronze armament of the Babylonian troops than were the bows and tomahawks of the Red Indians effective against Europeans' firearms. To succeed in defending their independence, peoples hitherto content with a neolithic equipment had to adopt arms of metal. That meant in practice that they had to learn metallurgy and adjust their economy to its requirements. It was not enough to purchase or steal some axes, spears, and helmets, manufactured in Babylonia: they must capture smiths to train armorers among their own people; they must produce surplus foodstuffs to support the new craftsmen and to secure the requisite raw materials; they must organize trade to ensure regular supplies. In a word, they must submit to the second revolution and adopt an urban economy.

The beginnings of metallurgy and of a rudimentary city life in Assyria may often be explained in this way. And not in Assyria only: in all the regions traversed by Sumerian trade routes and exposed to Sargon's campaigns—in North Syria, in Luristan, in Elam—we find centers of metallurgy arising soon after 3000 B.C. where Sumerian types were copied locally, and often modified according to local tastes. In one way or another Sumerian trade and the imperialism it inspired were propagating metallurgy and the new economy it implies.

Between 3000 and 2000 B.C. bronze-using civilizations were established in Crete, on the Greek mainland, at Troy on the Dardanelles, in the Kuban basin north of the Caucasus, on the plateau of Asia Minor, in Palestine and Syria, in Iran, and in Baluchistan. Each of these civilizations has a character of its own, but all exhibit so many concrete features of agreement with the products of Egypt, Sumer, or the Indus basin or of one of the secondary centers that their indebtedness to earlier foci of civilization is indisputable.

These secondary and tertiary civilizations are not original, but result from the adoption of traditions, ideas, and processes received by diffusion from older centers. In most cases the mechanism of this transmission is lost. The foregoing pages should reveal that effective mechanisms of diffusion were at work. The second revolution, once established, had to spread. And every village, converted into a city by the spread, became at once a new center of infection. Before 1500 B.C. the new industrial structure was reaching Spain, Britain, and Germany.

In less than five centuries more it had penetrated to Scandinavia and Siberia.

But in this process of diffusion culture was degraded. People who have learned a new technique are apt to apply it clumsily; proficiency requires generations of practice and of discipline. Again, the higher civilization is not adopted in its entirety; the recipient people feel the need of, and can assimilate, only a few items in the new cultural equipment. It is possible, for instance, to learn enough metallurgy and to get enough ore for armaments without learning to write or establishing such a commercial organization as should make writing indispensable. There thus arise different grades of civilization, varying degrees of approximation to the standards set by the primary centers. And these grades tend to be arranged in zones about the primary centers.

By 2500 B.C. the Minoans of Crete were dwelling in cities and living by industry and commerce. So intent are they, indeed, on profiting by the surplus wealth of Egypt and Syria, that they will build a city even on a tiny island with no cultivable land, provided it offer a convenient harbor. They had borrowed various items of the necessary technical equipment from Egypt or Sumer, directly or through Syria. They had early adopted the seal as a device for labeling their jars of oil and bales of merchandise. But the early native seals are rather crude products. Eventually they devised a rather clumsy pictographic script to assist them in their accountancy. They could smelt and work metals, and they employed the Sumerian type of axe-head with a hole for the shaft. But early Minoan metal tools look very clumsy beside the original models. Wheeled wagons were employed at first, but not the potters' wheel.

The Helladic people of Mainland Greece had begun to live in cities rather later than the Cretans, and were less dependent on trade and manufactures. They made no seals of their own, presumably because trade was on too small a scale for the device to be needed. Naturally they did not know how to write. Stone was still effectively competing with copper as tool material, and metal weapons were poor imitations of the Minoan.

Finally, the barbarians living north of the Balkans in what was to become the Austro-Hungarian Empire were only just beginning to use metal for weapons and ornaments, and occasionally for tools, by 2000 B.C. But they continued to live in small and nearly self-sufficing village communities. Of course they had no use for writing, or even for seals. Metallurgy they had learned from Greece and Troy, but they were far behind their masters. And their neighbors to the north were still neolithic!

CHAPTER VIII

THE REVOLUTION IN HUMAN KNOWLEDGE

THE economic revolution just described was possible only because Sumerians, Egyptians, and Indians disposed of a body of accumulated experience and applied science. The revolution inaugurated a new method of transmitting experience, fresh ways of organizing knowledge, and more exact sciences. The science requisite for the revolution had been transmitted in the form of craft lore by oral precept and example. The beginnings of writing and of mathematics and the standardization of weights and measures coincide in time with the revolution. The synchronism is not accidental. The practical needs of the new economy had, in fact, evoked the innovations.

In Sumer, we have seen, the resources needed to transform economic organization were accumulated in temples and administered by priests. The administrators were not isolated individuals, but continuing corporations. Nor were the temples isolated units. In the earliest historical times we find temples to the same deity in several Sumerian cities. The gods worshipped in them were not, or at least not exclusively, local deities; they were common to the whole land, like many of the saints to which Christian churches are dedicated. Presumably their priests too were not entirely restricted in their allegiance to the single city, but had a sort of international citizenship in "the kingdom of heaven" again like medieval clerics. Probably, though not certainly, these conditions go back to prehistoric times. The sovereignty of the same deities over the whole land would be the theologico-political counterpart of the uniformity of material culture throughout Sumer (and eventually throughout Babylonia).

A Sumerian temple disposed, as we have seen, of vast estates, flocks, and herds, and of huge revenues. It expended and augmented that wealth by assisting its votaries with advances and loans. Now the priests who administered that revenue must give an account to their divine master of their dealings with his property and must ensure the conservation and enrichment of his estates. They were confronted with a problem unprecedented in human history; never before had such vast wealth been concentrated under unitary control. To keep track of the god's dues and of his transactions the priest dare not rely on his memory. Nor would private mnemonic devices, like tying a knot in a handkerchief, help.[1] The individual priest was mortal, but the corporation to which he belonged was immortal, like the god it served. The priest might die before his master's loan had been repaid, but his duty of exacting repayment would be fulfilled by a colleague or successor. The god's minister must record how many jars of seed and of what quality he had advanced, how many sheep and of what breeds he had entrusted to a shepherd. And the transactions must be recorded in such a way that the priesthood, not just the priest, could interpret the record and secure satisfaction for the god. In a word, writing as a socially recognized system of recording was essential for keeping the temple accounts satisfactorily.

It will be recalled that in the first temple at Erech which signalized the transformation of the village into the city a primitive account-tablet was found. The symbols on it attest, if not a system of writing, at least a system of numeral notation. Rather later (but not later than 3000 B.C.) clay tablets bearing accounts are found not only at Erech, but also at Jemdet Nasr and other sites.

On the clay the priest has drawn characters and also numerals. The characters are mostly shorthand pictures—a jar, a bull's head, two triangles, and so on. The script is therefore termed pictographic. You can guess what the signs mean by simply looking at them. Even so they are already to some extent conventional. Society has selected and sanctioned one out of several possible ways of representing summarily, say, a bull. And some of the signs already mean more than the simple picture can indicate: the jar means a jar containing so much—in fact, a unit of measurement. Such a sign, standing for an idea, is termed an ideogram; its value is said to be ideographic (our mathematical symbols $+$, $-$, $\times$, $\div$, and so on are examples of ideograms).

Finally, there are already signs that cannot be recognized as depicting any specific object. The meaning of these ideograms is purely conventional. The priest has rightly despaired of indicating with a few strokes the distinction between several kinds of sheep. Instead he has adopted conventional signs to

---

[1] You know—it is to be hoped—what the knot meant, but a policeman, picking up your dead body, could not expect to guess which of the innumerable possible errands the knot had been designed to recall!

denote mouflon, urial, ram, wether, ewe. These signs are deliberate inventions by individual priests. But they must be accepted by the corporation, sanctioned by society to be useful.

Just because the accounts were not private documents and the signs were more than reminders to an individual, the system of writing employed had to be conventional. A canon of signs had to be established and authorized by society. In fact, we possess actual lists of signs as well as accounts from this period. And all administrators must be initiated into the convention. The process of initiation is what we call learning to read and write. (That consists, of course, in learning what meanings, *i.e.* sounds, the usage of our society attaches to twenty-six arbitrary symbols and learning to form the characters in the way approved by our fellows.) There must accordingly have been schools for scribes. The sign-lists which have been dug up could serve very well as school texts.

Moreover, since the same signs were employed both at Erech in Sumer and at Jemdet Nasr in Akkad, there must have been an interchange of pupils and masters between the various cities. The system of writing was not a convention peculiar to a particular temple-corporation, but was recognized and authorized by Sumerian society as a whole.

A large collection of tablets unearthed at Shuruppak (Fara) illustrates the development of Sumerian writing at the beginning of the historical period—after 3000 B.C. These documents are exclusively temple accounts and sign-lists used as school texts. In the latter the signs are grouped by subjects; different sorts of fish, for instance, are listed consecutively. And after each sign is added the name of the clerk or priest who invented it.

The signs are now highly conventionalized. The pictograms have been so simplified and abbreviated that the object intended is barely, if at all, recognizable. Moreover, signs are now used to represent sounds as well as ideas or things; they have become phonograms as well as, or instead of, ideograms.

The sign stood for bearded head and for the Sumerian

word *ka,* face. It may be now employed to denote just the syllable *ka,* without any reference to heads or faces. By selecting signs with the proper phonetic value it is now possible to spell out words—proper names or terms denoting concepts of actions that can hardly be represented by pictures. (In practice the above sign might also be used for "to speak," "to cry," "word," etc., and for the Sumerian equivalents *dug, gug, enim!*)

Signs continued, however, to be used with an ideographic value (to denote things or concepts instead of sounds) by themselves. And even when a word was spelt out phonetically an ideogram was often added to indicate to the reader the sort of word intended. Ideograms thus used are termed determinatives.

After 3000 B.C. we begin to find documents other than accounts, contracts, and sign-lists—at first mainly names and titles, then treaties, liturgical and historical texts, spells, and fragments of legal codes. And the script is further simplified; instead of being drawn, the various elements of the sign were stamped on to the soft clay with a wedge-shaped stylus. Because the signs are composed of wedge-shaped impressions, this classical Babylonian script is termed cuneiform. It remained in use till almost the beginning of our era, and was later adapted to write various foreign languages—Hittite (in Asia Minor), Vannic (in Armenia), Persian, and so on.

But even before 2500 B.C. the script, invented by the Sumerians, was being used to transcribe the language of their Semitic fellow-countrymen—Akkadian. This use of Sumerian characters to write Semitic names may have accelerated the conversion of ideographic into phonetic signs. But it complicated the result. A given sign is now liable to stand for one or more concepts, the sound of the Sumerian name of the concepts and the sound of the corresponding Semitic word. (The complexity is really much greater, since the same sign even in Sumerian might stand for several words, and so for several sounds.) Probably Sumerians and Babylonians never felt any difficulty here, but for modern scholars the transliteration of Sumerian names into European alphabets is always difficult, Ur-nina has been changed to Ur-nanshe, Ur-engur to Ur-nammu, and so on.

The fortunate circumstance that the Sumerians adopted clay as their writing material and made their documents imperishable by baking the clay, allows us to follow the history of writing from its very beginnings in Mesopotamia. It shows the development of writing and of city life advancing step by step. It is no accident that the oldest written documents in the world are accounts and dictionaries. They disclose the severely practical needs that prompted the invention of the Sumerian script.

Nowhere else can the practical economic origin of writing be demonstrated so clearly, because nowhere else can the art be traced to its starting point. Other peoples probably began writing on perishable materials and applied their script to inscriptions on more durable substances only when it was well advanced. The earliest Egyptian documents that survive are names and titles on sealings and vases, notes of accounts or inventories, and short records of events on slips of wood found in the royal tombs of the Ist and IInd Dynasties at Abydos. By this time (3000 or 2950 for the oldest) the system is already more mature than that of the oldest Sumerian documents. The signs are, indeed, quite recognizable pictures, and must originally have been pictograms. Indeed, in the early kings' names and titles, the pictures sometimes "come to life." And some characters retain their value as ideograms; indeed, as determinatives (p. 146), such were used throughout the whole period during which the Egyptian scripts were current.

But even in the days of Menes many picture-signs have a purely phonetic value, and words are regularly spelled out instead of being indicated by ideograms alone. The purely pictographic stage has been passed and remains a matter of inference. And quite soon the Egyptians were in possession of an alphabet: twenty-four signs have been adopted, each to stand for a single consonant (vowels were not written). But though any words could thus be spelt, ideograms and determinatives were never abandoned.

Of course even the picture-signs, though much more realistic than Sumerian pictograms, conform to a social convention. And in addition to this hieroglyphic script, the Egyptian scribes soon devised a quicker cursive hand (termed hieratic), the characters of which are so much simplified that the object once depicted is no longer recognizable.

The names, titles, and historical summaries that constitute the oldest surviving documents of Egyptian literature can hardly be used as evidence for the causes inspiring the invention of writing on the Nile. The practical uses of the art are attested from the time of the earliest dynasties. Scribes are explicitly mentioned among the royal officials. The observations on the height of the Nile and the assessments based thereon (p. 129) must have been written down. In later tomb-pictures (p. 133) we see the scribes busily scribbling down the rent or tribute brought in by tenants and herdsmen. In the workshop scenes they are recording the materials removed from store to be worked up by the individual artisans.

The scribes are officials, members of an organized and permanent public service. Their accounts and records must be intelligible to their colleagues, their superiors, and, in the last resort, to their supreme master, who is an earthly god. They must, as in Sumer, conform to a social convention; and reading and writing must be learned.

Nothing can be said of the Indus script, since only brief and undeciphered inscriptions on seals or copper tablets survive. It may here be noted that in Crete, where the Minoans began to develop a script before 2000 B.C., the vast majority of the extant documents are account tablets or inventories. The invention of writing was thus probably inspired everywhere, as in Sumer, by the peculiar practical needs of the urban economy. Admittedly the Sumerian script was invented, and at first used exclusively, by priests of a sort. But the Sumerian priests invented writing not in their capacity of ministers of superstition, but in that of administrators of a worldly estate. They, like the Egyptian and Minoan scribes, used the invention first not for magical and liturgical purposes, but for practical business and administration.

The invention of writing (as here defined) really marks an epoch in human progress. For us moderns it seems significant primarily because it offers an opportunity of penetrating to the very thoughts of our cultural ancestors, instead of trying to deduce those thoughts from their imperfect embodiments in deeds. But the true significance of writing is that it was destined to revolutionize the transmission of human knowledge. By its means a man can immortalize his experience and transmit it directly to contemporaries living far off and to generations yet unborn. It is the first step to raising science above the limits of space and time.

The utility of early scripts for this high mission must not be exaggerated. Writing was not invented as a medium of publication, but for the practical needs of administrative corporations. The earlier Sumerian and Egyptian scripts were distinctly clumsy instruments for expressing ideas. Even after a process of simplification lasting over 2000 years the cuneiform script employed between 600 and 1000 distinct characters. Before one could read or write, one had to memorize this formidable array of symbols and learn the complex rules for their combination. Egyptian hieroglyphic and hieratic scripts, despite their alphabetic elements, remained cumbered with a bewildering multitude of ideograms and determinatives, so that the number of characters required ran to about 500.

Under these conditions writing was inevitably a really difficult and specialized art that had to be learned by a long apprenticeship. Reading remained a mystery initiation into which was obtainable only by a prolonged schooling. Few possessed either the leisure or the talent to penetrate into the secrets of literature. Scribes were a comparatively restricted class in Oriental antiquity, like clerks in the Middle Ages. This class, it is true, never became a caste. Admission to the schools did not depend upon birth, though quite how scholars were selected is uncertain. But the "reading public" must have been a small minority in a vast population of illiterates.

Writing was, in fact, a profession, rather like metallurgy or weaving or war. But it was a profession that enjoyed a privileged position and offered prospects of advancement to office, power, and wealth. Literacy came thus to be valued not as a key to knowledge, but as a stepping-stone to prosperity and social rank. A rather hackneyed quotation from later Egyptian literature will illustrate an attitude that can hardly have been peculiar to the Nile Valley or the period of the texts.

An amusing group of Egyptian documents dating from the New Kingdom contrasts the prestige and privileges of a scribe with the hardships of a craftsman or a cultivator. They take the form of paternal admonitions, but embody sentiments that might be expressed today by a farmer or small shopkeeper writing to a son who has to choose between proceeding to higher education or entering industrial employment.

"Put writing in your heart that you may protect yourself from hard labor of any kind and be a magistrate of high repute. The scribe is released from manual tasks; it is he who commands. . . . Do you not hold the scribe's palette? That is what makes the difference between you and the man who handles an oar.

"I have seen the metal-worker at his task at the mouth of his furnace with fingers like a crocodile's. He stank worse than fish-spawn. Every workman who holds a chisel suffers more than the men who hack the ground; wood is his field and the chisel his mattock. At night when he is free, he toils more than his arms can do (? at overtime work); even at night he lights (his lamp to work by). The stonecutter seeks work in every hard stone; when he has done the great part of his labor his arms are exhausted, he is tired out. . . . The weaver in a workshop is worse off than a woman; (he squats) with his knees to his belly and does not taste (fresh) air. He must give loaves to the porters to see the light."

The prospects of social advancement implied in these admonitions may not have been so bright or definite at earlier periods or in other countries. But the general attitude towards clerical employments and theoretical science as contrasted to manual labor and applied sciences probably goes back to the earliest phases of urban life, and was the same in Sumer as in Egypt. The foregoing quotations accordingly recall the fact that the second revolution had produced or accentuated a division of society into classes. In practice kings, priests, nobles, and generals stand opposed to peasants, fishermen, artisans, and laborers. And in this class division the scribes belong to the former class; writing is a "respectable" profession.

Now material progress in prehistoric times had been due mainly to improvements in technique, made presumably by the craftsmen and husbandmen themselves. But in the class division of urban society scribes belong to the "upper classes," in contrast to the working artisans and farmers; writing is a respectable profession while farming, metallurgy, and carpentry are not. The practical applied science of botany, chemistry, and geology were not accordingly embraced in the literary tradition whose exponents looked down upon manual labor; craft lore was not reduced to writing nor handed on in book form.

On the other hand, certain sciences and pseudo-sciences— mathematics, surgery, medicine, astrology, alchemy, haruspicy —were made the subjects of written treatises. They thus formed a body of learned sciences, accessible only to those who had been initiated into the mysteries of reading and writing. But by this very fact the disciplines in question were liable to be divorced from practical life. In entering the school the pupil turned his back on the plow and the bench; he had no desire to return to them.

Inevitably, too, words written with such difficulty and deciphered so laboriously must seem to possess an authority of their own. The immortalization of a word in writing must have seemed a supernatural process; it was surely magical that a man long vanished from the land of the living could still speak from a clay tablet or a papyrus roll. Words thus spoken must possess a kind of *mana*. Thus learned men in the East, like schoolmen in our own Middle Ages, were apt to turn to books in preference to Nature. In Egypt books on mathematics, surgery, and medicine, composed under the Old Kingdom (before 2400 B.C.) were slavishly, and often very incompetently, copied after 2000. Between 800 and 600 B.C. the upstart kings of Assyria were at pains to acquire for their libraries copies of texts going back to the time of Hammurabi (about 1800 B.C.) or of Sargon of Agade (2350).

Instead of demanding that a book should be up to date and embody the latest discoveries, the Egyptian or Babylonian student valued it for its antiquity. A publisher would then advertise his wares not as a "new and revised edition," but as a faithful copy of a fabulously old text. And so the "jacket" of the Rhind Mathematical Papyrus runs: "Rules for enquiring into nature and for knowing all that exists. The roll was written in the thirty-third year of King Aauserre in the likeness of a writing of antiquity made in the time of king Nemare (1880-1850 B.C.). It was the scribe Ahmose who made this copy." One of the treatises included in the Ebers Medical Papyrus is entitled "The Book of Healing Illnesses found in ancient writing in a chest at the feet of Anubis in the time of King Usaphaïs" (a monarch of Dynasty I).

Nevertheless the schools for scribes did actually function as what we should call research institutes. Even for the purposes of teaching it was necessary to organize and systematize the knowledge to be imparted. The post of instructor gave opportunities and inducements for addition to knowledge by a sort of "theoretical research."

Particularly in Mesopotamia the very "scholastic" attitude, just criticized, promoted the systematic organization of learning. From 2500 B.C. onwards people of Semitic speech were winning the upper hand in Babylonia. The First Dynasty of Babylon that finally unified Sumer and Akkad about 1800 was Semitic. And so Semitic Akkadian thereafter became the official language of the kingdom. Sumerian became a dead language. But the revered old texts were written in Sumerian. And Sumerian remained the language of religion, just as Latin did in medieval Europe. The priests of the temples, retaining their corporate identity from prehistoric Sumerian times, were trained in the Sumerian tradition whatever their native speech might have been before ordination.

Naturally they held that the ancient gods of the land must still be conciliated with Sumerian liturgies; the old magic powers could be compelled only with Sumerian spells. The temple schools had therefore now to teach and study Sumerian, just as medieval colleges had to study Latin. In addition to instruction in reading and writing, they had to provide for some at least of their students a "higher education" and to study subjects of no practical utility in mundane affairs. In the course of this study they learned to make grammars and dictionaries to facilitate the comprehension and correct recitation of the old Sumerian hymns and incantations and to collect and arrange the ancient texts. Though inspired by hopes of supernatural gain, this work did give scholars training in the organization of knowledge and in research; and it has enabled us to read Sumerian.

Even in Egypt the reverence for ancient traditions going back to the glorious Pyramid Age, attested in the titles we quoted on pp. 150-1, impelled later generations to the systematic study of documents composed in a language and a script further removed from contemporary usage than are those of Chaucer's days from our own.

And in neither country was the scribe's education confined to reading and writing. To fulfil the functions normally required of him, the scribe must study mathematics too. Some must have been trained also in astrology, medicine, surgery, and perhaps even alchemy. The bulk of the papyri and tablets which modern scholars designate "mathematical," "medical," or in general "scientific," have probably been produced and used in such schools. To these we may add accounts and field-plans, calendars, and other documents illustrating applications of arithmetic, geometry, astronomy, and so on. From these sources we have to deduce how ancient learning was organized, how it was transmitted, and what it had achieved.

Accounts and calendars obviously bear precisely the same relation to the science of mathematics as do metal slags and castings to the science of chemistry. From each we can infer the amount of scientific knowledge the accountant or the metallurgist was actually applying in the course of his business. Field-plans are not differentiated from the material handled by the "prehistoric archaeologist" by the fact that they have figures and words written in.

Secondly, there are included in the "scientific" texts themselves various tables comparable to our multiplication and interest tables. These are, of course, helps to reckoning and instruments of calculation. Though the extant examples are mostly drawn up for use in "schools," they are strictly comparable to the instruments used by a craftsman in the application of his branch of science. Multiplication tables fulfil the same function as furnaces, crucibles, and bellows. The insight they give into mathematical knowledge is of precisely the same order as that which can be obtained into applied chemistry from an examination of uninscribed archaeological relics.

The remaining texts, however, have no exact counterparts in the material which pure archaeology uses as illustrations of applied sciences. These documents are the actual instruments in the transmission of scientific knowledge. They take the place of textbooks for school use, books of reference, and perhaps communications in learned journals amongst us. But they are strikingly unlike modern textbooks that aim at explaining the general theory and methods of a whole discipline, and equally unlike the monographs which aim at the exposition and demonstration of a particular discovery or generalization.

The mathematical texts are simply concrete examples of different problems worked out in full. They illustrate to the reader how to do sums of various kinds. But by themselves such series of examples could hardly suffice to enlighten a novice as to new methods nor impart to him fresh knowledge.

They must have been intended as supplements to oral instruction. The same is true of the medical texts. They contain at best a summary of symptoms, recapitulated in a diagnosis, and followed by a prescription. They thus resemble the notes of cases a student would take during his hospital practice. They presuppose some sort of oral instruction given by the professor.

It looks then as if there was no real distinction between the transmission of the learned sciences and that of the applied sciences or crafts; the sort of instruction given to a student of mathematics or medicine was essentially the same as that given to an apprentice in metallurgy or weaving. The apprentice watches his master at work, is shown how to perform the operation, and is then set to work himself under his master's eye to be corrected when he goes wrong. Just in the same way, the pupil scribe or doctor in Egypt and Babylonia must have watched his professor working out simple examples of treating actual cases. Literature gives no hint that this practical instruction was preceded or supplemented by a reasoned exposition of general principles and abstract theory such as today distinguishes a university training, in engineering, say, from mere apprenticeship.

The learned sciences in the Ancient East were still more obviously allied to the crafts in their aims. Egyptian and Babylonian mathematics, medicine, and astrology professedly aimed at satisfying specific needs felt by Egyptian and Babylonian societies. They aimed at solving problems actually arising in the course of business and building, at the cure of known diseases, and at the determination of agricultural seasons, and still more the prediction of men's fortunes.

Mathematics is as obviously a consequence of the economic needs of the urban revolution as is writing. The business transactions of temple corporations and revenue administration by a public service need standardized weights and measures, a system of numerical notation, and rules to expedite counting, as much as they need writing.

Measurement, of course, did not begin with the revolution. It only means comparing objects in respect to length, width, weight, and so on. In some form it must be as old as human industry. You cannot fit a string to a bow nor an axe-head to its shaft without measurement. At first the objects to be fitted were compared directly one to the other. As soon as industrial operations became more complicated, it was more convenient to compare each part to one standard. In boat-building it would be inconvenient to have to compare each plank you were cutting with the keel already laid down and with the last plank cut. It was easier to compare the keel with, say, your arm, and cut each plank to the number of arm's lengths represented in the keel.

At first the standards would be individual natural objects. Your finger, your palm, and your forearm (eel or cubit) provided, as it were, personal units of length. In exchanges a grain of barley or a sackful of grain would be treated as a unit of weight. But for social labor that requires both accuracy and the co-operation of several workers personal measures prove inadequate; no two workers need have arms of precisely the same length. So too in exchanging quantities the varying weights of different barley-grains and disproportion in the content of sacks may cause injustice. Weights and measures have to be standardized. That is, society must agree to assign a fixed value to the finger, the span, and the cubit, the grain and the sackful. The social standards of length are then marked on measuring rods; weights of stone or metal are made to represent the convenient grain and sackful. Soon it is arranged that the several conventional units of length, volume, weight, and so on shall bear simple mathematical relations to each other, though retaining their old names. The cubit is chosen as a simple multiple of the span, and so on. Standardization of weights and measures, therefore, like language and writing, reposes on a convention. Weights and measures, like words and characters, have to be authorized by social usage.

Incidentally, measurement by conventional standards is more abstract than the comparison of concrete individual objects. And all measurement involves abstract thinking. In measuring lengths of stuffs you ignore their materials, colors, patterns, textures, and so on, to concentrate on length. Ultimately the process leads to concepts of "pure quantity" and "Euclidean space."

It must not be supposed that ancient societies were interested in infinite length or empty space. Their abstractions were limited by practical interests. The ancient Sumerian measures of area have in some cases the same names as measures of weight; in particular the smallest unit in both "tables" is the še or grain, in other words, Sumerian "square measure" was originally a seed measure. The Sumerian's interest was the quantity of seed needed to sow his field. He regarded the field not as occupying so much "empty space," but as needing so much seed-grain. With the areas of bits of uncultivable desert or blue sky he was not concerned.

Weighing, it may be remarked, required also the invention of a special instrument, the balance. Objects supposed by Petrie to be weights have been discovered in prehistoric Egyptian graves. If Petrie be right, it must be admitted that the invention of the balance and standardization of weights began some time before the revolution.

That is intrinsically probable. In any case, the several communities among whom the revolution was traced in Chapter VIII came to attach rather different conventional values to their several units. After the revolution, that is, we find different systems of weights and measures in Egypt, Mesopotamia, and India. Even in Mesopotamia itself minor differences in weights may be due to the adoption of divergent standards in several autonomous cities. Trade was, however, sufficiently international for the standards of one country to find recognition and usage in another. So the Egyptian sometimes measured by Babylonian units of weight instead of the native weights.

Counting must go back to the earliest human societies, though some savages today cannot, it is alleged, count beyond five. Presumably men began by counting on their fingers. Hence the widespread decimal system whereby numbers from one to ten have distinct names.

In all cases, of course, men were numbering actual objects—salmon caught, sheep in a fold, threads in the weft, and so on. The modest totals that a paleolithic hunter or a neolithic herdsman might want to remember could be recorded by notches on a stick. For recording the vast revenues of a Sumerian temple or an Egyptian pharaoh such series of strokes became too cumbersome. The priestly corporation and the civil service had to adopt a conventional system for noting down large quantities. Both in Sumer and in Egypt there are documents, using a conventional system of numeration, that are older than the earliest extant examples of writing.

In both countries and also in India (and subsequently in Crete) the conventions adopted for recording large totals were substantially the same. Units were represented by one sign repeated as often as necessary to denote any number up to 9. A different symbol was adopted to denote 10 and multiples of 10, and so with the next higher units. In Egypt the following symbols are attested as early as Dynasty I: $|$ $=$ 1; $\cap$ = 10; @ = 100; $\frac{\mathrm{S}}{}$ = 1000. In Mesopotamia the system developed along different lines.

On the oldest account tablets from Erech and Jemdet Nasr, the following numerals occur; D = 1, 0 = 10, O = 100. But in other texts from the same cities, probably rather later, the numerals have the following values: D = 1, 0 = 10, D = 60, O = 600. This is the so-called sexagesimal system used by the Sumerians and then by the Babylonians as long as their civilization survived. Naturally, the forms of the numerals were simplified in the course of time, as in Egypt. But in Babylonia this simplification had surprising consequences.

When the imprint of a wedge-shaped stylus took the place of drawn signs in the script D became ▼, o became ⟨ , D ▼, and O 𝕯 or (in the "mathematical texts" ◊· Hence by about 2000 B.C. the same sign represented any power of sixty (including one) and ten such units respectively. Only the order of the signs helped distinguish their values: ▼▼ ⟨ ⟨ ⟨▼ must mean 2 × 60 + 3 × 10 + 1, or, in our notation, 151. The Babylonians thus found themselves in possession of a system using "place value" just like our own. It had one defect: there was no sign for zero; but some time after 1000 B.C. this deficiency was made good.

All these systems are rather clumsy; to write 879 in Egyptian, for instance, twenty-four distinct signs had to be drawn. On the other hand, addition and subtraction are almost as easy as in counting on the fingers: ||| added to ⫴ evidently make ⫽⫽. Multiplication and division by 10 are also easily represented. To multiply 2 by 10 merely involved changing ▼▼ to ⟨⟨.

Our oldest "mathematical documents," the pictographic account tablets, illustrate only the simplest mathematical operations. They record numbers of actual sheep, measures of barley, or jugs of beer. Totals are reached by addition and subtraction. The areas of fields (in the sense defined on p. 154) are reckoned as the product of two sides. Under such conditions fractions need not arise. The scribe is counting real sheep and men. An eighth of a sheep and five-eighths of a man would be meaningless. In dealing with measures and volumes, the several units, each with distinct names, took the place of fractions, as elementary arithmetic expresses fractions of a pound in ounces, pennyweights, grains, etc. So in Sumer convention had fixed the values of the "natural units" of length so that 15 fingers made 1 span, 2 spans 1 cubit, and so on. Both in Sumerian and Egyptian writing, simple numerals, unaccompanied by any other sign or word, might be used to denote units of weight or of length: so in Sumerian D might stand for 1 gan and 0 for 1 bur (*i.e.* 18 gan). Perhaps from this sort of practice arose "individual signs" used to denote certain fractions: in Egyptian ⊂ for ½″, (x = ¼) ♀ ⅓, and ♀ ⅔; in Babylonian ✛ for ½″, ⊞ ⅓ and ⫟ ⅔.

But the complexities introduced into social life by the urban revolution raised problems that required more advanced mathematical processes for a satisfactory solution. Large armies of laborers were gathered together to execute gigantic public works, and provision must be made for these in advance. It was necessary to calculate the supplies of food and raw material that must be collected; the time likely to be occupied had accordingly to be estimated. But that might involve reckoning up the cubic contents of sloping banks of earth or of pyramids or the number of bricks in the walls of a well. The wages of gangs had to be apportioned in accordance with the qualifications or output of each member.

Grain was stored up in granaries that might be cylindrical or pyramidal in shape; still, the overseers and revenue officers needed to know how much grain to expect from such containers. Trade was organized on a partnership basis, and the profits had to be apportioned according to the shares contributed. A Sumerian deity was daily placated with large offerings of beer, the strength of which was prescribed by ritual usage. The temple brewer needed to know the quantities of grain requisite for the malting and for the actual liquor, and the overseer must ascertain how much grain to issue to him for each purpose and for each brew. Egyptian superstition demanded extreme accuracy in the erection of pyramids; the mason must know the exact measures of the individual blocks that must be cut to face such monuments.

The sort of problem which an Egyptian scribe might have to solve is stated in a late papyrus, dating from about 1200 B.C. The speaker is supposed to be upbraiding a rival for incompetence:—

"You say: 'I am the scribe who issues commands to the levy.' You are given a reservoir to dig. But you come to me to inquire about the rations for the soldiers and say: 'Reckon it out.' You desert your office and the burden of teaching it to you falls on me.

"You are the clever scribe at the head of the levy. A ramp is to be constructed, 730 cubits long, 55 cubits wide, containing 120 compartments and filled with reeds and beams. . . . The quantity of bricks required for it is demanded of the generals, and the scribes are gathered together without one of them knowing anything. They put their trust in you saying: 'You are the clever scribe, my friend! . . . Answer us, how many bricks are needed for it?'

"It is said to you, 'Empty the magazine that has been filled with sand under your lord's monument that has been brought from the Red Mountain. It measured 30 cubits when lying extended on the ground and 20 cubits in breadth. The magazine consisted of several divisions each 50 cubits high. You are commissioned to find out how many men will demolish it in six hours.' "

(The problems are, of course, insoluble as stated, but that is part of the jest here.)

It is problems of just the foregoing kinds that are worked out in the extant mathematical texts from Egypt and Babylonia. Most of the problems seem to us rather trivial; few should seriously perplex an elementary school boy today. But it would be grossly unfair to judge scribes who lived 5000 years ago by modern standards. Operations that worried them are familiar to us just because we have, through the Greeks and Arabs, inherited the techniques they devised.

Actually the Sumerian and Egyptian scribes were experimenting in an utterly strange and uncharted domain, opened up by the unprecedented events of the urban revolution. The problems they had to solve were absolutely new, and had never arisen before because they were created by the revolution itself. Like the rest of its results, they are familiar as the very basis of our own civilization. But the ancient mathematician had actually to invent methods for their solution.

In the first place, they had to create the machinery for reckoning. The first step had been to devise a system of notation, to reduce to writing whole numbers for which, after all, names already existed in spoken language. The next step was to improve the technique of reckoning. Addition and subtraction are simply counting abbreviated by memorizing results already obtained. In "adding" 5 to 3 we just remember that the result (presumably first obtained by counting) is 8, instead of counting up step by step. As already remarked, the Egyptian and Sumerian notation gave graphic expression to this fact.

Multiplication is a further abbreviation of addition. To multiply 5 by 3 means to add three 5's together. We learn at school that the result is 15. The Egyptians do not seem to have recorded this result as something to be memorized. In any case, they never applied the process familiar to us. They always proceeded by the method of "duplication." They added the multiplicand to itself. But they did remember that $12 + 12$ (i.e. 12×2) $= 24$, and abbreviated the process to that extent. An example illustrates the method. This is how the Egyptians would work out 12×12 and 14×80:—

	1	12		1	80
	2	24	V	10	800
V	4	48		2	160
V	8	96	V	4	320

Total	144	Total	1120

(You write 1 opposite the multiplicand, and then double each side till in the first column you have numbers totalling up to the multiplier, ticking off the relevant lines. You then add up the corresponding figures in the second column. In example 2 the process is simplified by the decimal notation as described on p. 156.

In division the process is reversed. The division of 19 by 8, which the Egyptian would have expressed as "reckoning with 8 to find 19," would be thus set out:—

$$
\begin{array}{rcc}
 & 1 & 8 \\
\vee & 2 & 16 \\
 & \overline{2} & \overline{4} \\
\vee & \overline{4} & 2 \\
\vee & \overline{8} & 1 \\
\end{array}
$$

result $2 + \overline{4} + \overline{8}$

(Here he doubles and halves the divisor until numbers in the second column add up to the dividend, ticking off the integers and fractions in the first column and adding together the ticked figures $1/2$, $1/4$ can be written, $\overline{2}$, $\overline{4}$, in conformity with Egyptian fractional notation.)

It is probable that the Sumerians first used similar "additive" methods. But before 2000 B.C. the Babylonians were familiar with multiplication as we know it. That means that they possessed multiplication tables, and such have come down to us. They had, that is, noted down the results obtained by additive methods and tabulated them for memorization or reference. They had thus equipped themselves with instruments for ready reckoning, and thereby enormously lightened and accelerated the work of calculation.

Possibly it was the great importance of trade for Babylonia that evoked this simplification of arithmetical procedure. Mesopotamia had been more dependent than Egypt on foreign trade in prehistoric times and remained so. Her geographical position makes her a junction of natural trade routes, whereas Egypt is relatively isolated. The transaction of foreign business on a large scale would certainly have been expedited by the new procedure. At the same time the compilation of the tables, *i.e.*, the systematic recording and arrangement of results obtained by simpler reckonings, may be credited to the "research organization" of the temple schools.

The extant tables give the product of the multiplier with all integers up to 20 and with 30, 40, and 50 too, and are set out and arranged like ours. But the multipliers include also seemingly high numbers like 1,15 and even 44,26,40 (all, of course, expressed in sexagesimal notation). They could therefore serve also as division tables, as explained below. Tables of squares, cubes, and other powers, square roots, cube roots, etc., also survive.

Evidently the practical problems that confronted the scribes, such as even the division of rations among workmen, must eventually have forced them to deal with fractional quantities. To comprehend what that meant, it is well to recall how fractions bothered us in our early schooldays. To Egyptians and Babylonians they were something absolutely novel. You cannot conveniently represent fractions, as you can integers, on the fingers or an abacus. A notation had to be devised for quantities which could not be thus concretely imaged.

The Egyptians denoted fractions (with numerator 1) by a sign over the denominator, which may be represented in our notation by a stroke. (There were, of course, special signs for 1/2, 1/3, and 2/3 as noted.) It would clearly be difficult on this notation to write 2/5 or 7/10. And, in fact, the Egyptians never wrote such fractions at all. They always expressed them as a sum of fractions with numerator 1, or, as we should say, of aliquot parts, save that 2/3 might be introduced into the series. Our examples are accordingly resolved as follows: $2/5 = 1/3 + 1/15$ (or, in Egyptian notation, $\overline{3} + \overline{15}$) and $7/10 = 2/3 + 1/30$. Tables were compiled giving the correct resolution of all fractions whose numerator is 2 and whose denominator is an odd number from 3 to 101. The first part of the Rhind Papyrus sets forth this table with "working out" attached.

The Egyptians had then hardly grasped that fractions were amenable to precisely the same rules as integers. The failure was due primarily to their primitive technique of reckoning; division carried out on the Egyptian plan automatically results in just such series of aliquot parts. Defective notation was a contributory cause in perpetuating the usage.

The transformation of the numeral system, described on p. 156, incidentally gave Babylonian mathematicians a complete mastery of fractional quantities about 2000 B.C. The simplification of the script meant that the value of a numeral depended entirely upon its position relative to others. With us the same figure, 5, is used to denote $5 \times 10, 5 \times 1, 5/10$, and so on. Which value it possesses is determined in each given case by its position relative to other figures including zero and decimal point. Just so about 2000 B.C. the Babylonians came in mathematical texts to use the same group of signs ≪ to denote 20 and 20/60; but they lacked signs for 0 and . and used a sexagesimal scale. Thereby they were enabled to extend the mastery of numbers to the whole domain of the rational. For they could express fractions just as we do in "decimals": 1/5 could be written ;12 (it is convenient for us to insert a ; to represent the "point" that the Babylonians lacked), 2/5 ;24, and so on. And they treated their sexagesimal fractions exactly like integers.

This notation simplified the difficult operation of division. They drew up tables of the reciprocals of numbers between 1 and 60:—

2	30	5	12
3	20	6	10
4	15	8	7;30, and so on.

Thereafter instead of dividing by, say, 5, you multiplied by its reciprocal ;12 (12/60). But what happened when the reciprocal was not a finite number—60/7, for instance—is unknown.

The system of sexagesimal fractions and the new processes thereby initiated were incidental consequences of a change in the script. But the realization of its potentialities and their exploitation were achievements apparently of the temple schools. The system seems, in fact, confined to the "mathematical texts" compiled in and for such schools. It was, however, used in the earliest texts for the solution of problems in architecture and military engineering and for calculating interest and principal. Apparently only a thousand years later was the new mathematic applied to astronomical calculations, despite the importance of astrology in the temple curricula.

To teach and apply the new methods of reckoning it was desirable to adopt conventionally standardized terms for the several operations; to make mathematics a science an exact terminology was essential. The definition of terms is, of course, a social function, and the schools were the institutions to select the expression that should alone be accepted as the designation or indicator of each operation. As far as Egypt is concerned, there is considerable variation in the Rhind Papyrus in the expressions used to denote addition, subtraction, and so on; multiply 5 by 4 may be expressed "count with 4 5 times," "reckon with 4 5 times." In the Moscow Papyrus the terminology is less variable, but not yet quite fixed.

The Babylonian texts, on the other hand, from 2000 B.C. employ a very explicit terminology. Indeed, the Babylonians were well on the way to creating a mathematical symbolism that would materially accelerate calculation. First, the technical terms for several operations were words of one syllable expressed by a single cuneiform sign. Then the Babylonians, though they spoke a Semitic tongue, used the old Sumerian terms for operations like "multiplied by," "find the reciprocal of." Finally, many of the technical words were written as ideograms instead of being spelt out. (Our arithmetical and geometrical symbols $+, \times, \Delta, \pi$ are, of course, true ideograms.) The later the texts, and therefore the deader the Sumerian language, the more Sumerian terms and ideograms were used. They became quite abstract symbols freed from the concrete notions of "nodding the head" or "breaking away" that inhere in Egyptian terms. But, even in Egyptian, ideograms were sometimes employed as mathematical symbols; in the Rhind Papyrus a pair of legs may denote $+$ or $-$, according to the direction of the feet.

The terminology for what we regard as ratios was curious. Babylonian and Egyptian texts frequently refer to the "batter"

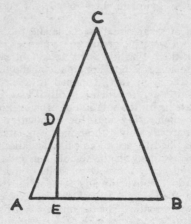

FIG. 9.—DIAGRAM TO ILLUSTRATE THE FORMULA FOR "BATTER."

or "slope" of a pyramid's sides. We should express this as a ratio, as we say 1 in 10 for the gradient of a hill. The Egyptians always express this as a length, e.g., 5-1/25 palms. What they really meant was 5-1/25 palms horizontally for each cubit of height or, as we should say, "AE/ED, where ED is one unit of length, a cubit." The Babylonian expressed this more clearly: "for 1 cubit, 1 the batter-value" (always reckoned in GAR). Both phrases illustrate how very concrete mathematical thinking remained.

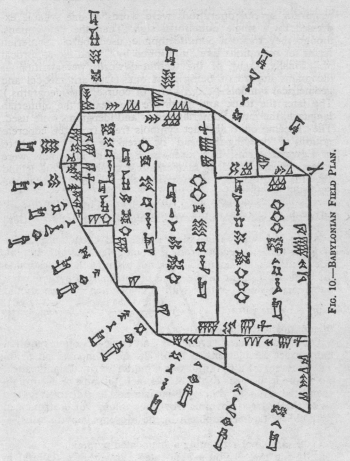

FIG. 10.—BABYLONIAN FIELD PLAN.

The conditions of urban economy, indicated on pp. 156-7, required some knowledge of geometrical relations. The areas of fields must be determined for estimations of the seed required for sowing them and the rent or tax that might be exacted in respect of them. But for such estimates and assessments absolute accuracy was unnecessary: the bailiff only wanted to know roughly how much grain to allow for each field; the tax-collector needed a general idea of the yield to be expected. We have seen that even before 3000 B.C. the Sumerians were calculating the areas of fields as the product of length by breadth; they were, that is, applying the correct geometrical formula for the area of a rectangle.

In later documents the areas of irregular quadrangles are calculated by various approximations, usually the mean of the products of the two pairs of adjacent sides. Polygonal fields were divided up into quadrangles and triangles, the areas of which were similarly calculated. In Egypt, even in New Kingdom contracts, the area of a four-sided field is taken as half the sum of two adjacent sides multiplied by half the sum of the remaining sides. In the case of a triangular field the lengths of two sides were added together and halved, and then multiplied by half the length of the third side.

The documents just examined generally contain plans of the fields in question. The lengths are written in along the sides, but the plans are not drawn accurately or to scale. The theory that exact geometry arose out of land-surveying in Egypt or Babylonia is not supported by the evidence at our disposal.

Again, it would be useful as a check to know the quantity of grain to be expected from a rectangular silo with sloping sides, but absolute accuracy was not essential. So, to estimate the contents of a pit in the form of a truncated pyramid, the Babylonians were content with a calculation that we should express by the formula $V = h \left[\dfrac{(a + b)^2}{2} + \dfrac{(a - b)^2}{2} \right]$, though this formula is incorrect.

On the other hand, architects and engineers often required more exact calculations to fulfill the tasks imposed on them. The accuracy of a pyramid was a matter of ritual significance. To secure it the sizes of the blocks facing it must be accurately calculated. And so the Egyptian scribes had discovered and used the correct formula for the volume of a truncated pyramid. A famous problem in the Moscow Papyrus runs:—

"Example of reckoning a ?truncated pyramid.

If one says to you a ?truncated pyramid of 6 (cubits) in height to 4 (cubits) on the underside to 2 (cubits) on the upper side.

Reckon with this 4 squared, it gives 16.

Double 4, it gives 8.

Reckon with this 2 squared; it gives 4.

Add together this 16 to this 8 and to this 4. It gives 28.

Reckon 1/3 of 6; it gives 2. Reckon with 28 2 times; it gives 56.

See: 56 it is. You have got the answer."

The process here set out can be expressed $V = 1/3$ (a^2 +

$ab + b^2$)—the correct formula for the frustum of a pyramid. The rough figure accompanying the example suggests an irregular pyramid—in fact, one of the blocks casing a regular pyramid (Fig. 11).

Problems involving the relation of the circumference to the diameter of a circle, the "irrational" quantity which we call π, inevitably arose. In their solution the Babylonians were content with a very rough approximation, $\pi = 3$, presumably obtained by direct measurement. The Egyptians, on the other hand, used a surprisingly close approximation in estimating the area of circles. An example in the Rhind Papyrus runs:—

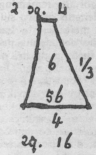

FIG. 11.—EXACT COPY OF FIGURE FROM MOSCOW PAPYRUS, REVERSED AND WITH SYMBOLS TRANSLITERATED.

"Method of reckoning a circular piece of land of diameter 9 *khet*. What is its area?

You are to subtract 1/9 of it, namely 1. Remainder 8.

You are to reckon with 8 8 times; it becomes 64. This is its area in land: 6 thousands-of-land and 4 *setat*."

The formula used is $(d = 1/9)^2$, which makes $\pi = (16/9)^2$. The result of Pythagoras' Theorem (that in a right-angled triangle the square on the side opposite the right angle is equal to the sum of the squares on the other two sides) was perfectly familiar to the Babylonians from 2000 B.C. Of course, they could not apply it in all calculations, since they could not handle surds. When the sum of the two squares yielded a number that was not itself a perfect square, they had to resort to other methods of obtaining an approximate result. A tablet in Berlin gives two calculations of the diagonal of a door ;40 GAR high and ;10 GAR wide. They give respectively values of ;41,15 and ;42,13, 20, and can be represented by the formulas $d = h + \dfrac{w^2}{2h}$ and $d = h + 2w^2h$. The first formula is the arithmetical mean between two approximations to the value of $\sqrt{h^2 + w^2}$.

In Egypt there is no direct evidence for the application of Pythagoras' Theorem. The oft-repeated statement that a triangle with sides 3, 4, and 5 was used in laying out a right angle is quite unfounded.

The Babylonians could even calculate the height of an arc,

given the length of its chord and the circle's diameter. Their actual procedure can be expressed by the formula $h = \frac{1}{2} (d - \sqrt{d^2 - a^2})$, and is perfectly correct. It implies appreciation of the properties of similar triangles, but not, of course, that Babylonians had worked out the various steps in pure geometry by which the formula is deduced by Euclid.

In fact, we do not know how any of the foregoing geometrical rules were obtained. They certainly had not been deduced *a priori* from the properties of abstract space as they purport to be in Euclid's geometry. For such a "pure geometry" there is no evidence at all. Figures often accompany the geometrical problems in the mathematical papyri and tablets, but such figures are no more drawn to scale than are the field-plans in contracts. On the other hand, the patterns decorating craft-products, piles of bricks, and composite wooden boxes often give very striking ocular demonstrations of geometrical propositions. Checker patterns, that arise almost spontaneously in basketry and matting, illustrate concretely the geometrical formula for the area of a rectangle. Incidentally, painted checker patterns were popular on vases precisely at the time of the earliest pictographic tablets on which the Sumerians applied this formula.

Early Oriental decorative art was very largely geometric. Patterns of triangles and checkers in textiles or mosaic might easily illustrate Pythagoras' Theorem. Designs based on intersecting circles or on squares and triangles inscribed in circles were very popular, and might show how to calculate the height of an arc. But these patterns are produced by artists and craftsmen, not mathematicians.

Nor do the mathematical texts ever enunciate a general rule or formula. No rule is stated for finding the area of a rectangle or a circle nor the volume of a cylinder or truncated pyramid. There is no statement beyond the actual working out as given in the two Egyptian examples cited. No text gives any more explanation of the reason for the operations than is contained in the quoted problems. Indeed, the quantities dealt with are seldom even pure numbers, but generally so many loaves or cubits or bushels.

The mathematical texts, in fact, consist entirely of concrete problems of the sort likely to arise in real life worked out step by step, like the examples in a school arithmetic. And, as in a school arithmetic, the actual values in the problems have been so selected that a neat result can be obtained by the methods at the disposal of the scribe: the circles' diameters are always divisible exactly by 9, the quadratics do not lead to surds. The examples do not illustrate how the deductions of a pure mathematics could be applied to problems of everyday life. They illustrate rather methods whereby problems arising in practice had been satisfactorily solved.

Nevertheless, the activity that produced our mathematical texts was not confined to recording problems that had been put to the scribe and his methods of solving these. Still less did it consist merely of making simplified versions of such problems for the instruction of beginners. The examples look as if they had been deliberately constructed. They give the impression that scholars in higher centers of learning were setting themselves problems just to see what they could do neatly. In that way they would be building up techniques which were later applied not only to the familiar tasks dealt with in the examples, but also to those confronting other colleagues, like astrologers.

To this extent the Babylonian mathematical tablets at least disclose as strictly "theoretical" a science as any paper presented to the Royal Society. It was theoretical in the sense that it resulted from investigations each of which was not deliberately directed to the solution of any specific practical problem. But as a whole the problems investigated were strictly modeled on the actual real-life problems from which they started. Indeed, it looks as if the research they disclose was really limited in its scope by consciously conceived possibilities of practical application. In any case, no attempt was made to generalize the results.

It would help us to estimate the scientific value of Egyptian and Babylonian mathematics if we knew exactly how the results of investigations were arranged. In a scientific arithmetic the examples would today be grouped according to the methods employed, irrespective of whether the problems concerned grocers, builders, surveyors, or generals. The existing material gives little indication of the principles of arrangement followed in Egypt and Babylonia. In the Moscow Papyrus no systematic arrangement at all is recognizable. The examples in the Rhind Papyrus are deliberately grouped as follows:—

i.   Problems 1-6. Division of 10 loaves between 1, 2, 6, 7, 8, and 9 men.

ii. 7-20. "Completions": multiplication of vulgar and improper fractions.

iii. 21-23. "Completions": subtraction of fractions.

iv. 24-38. Simple equations.

v. 39-40. Division of loaves in unequal proportions.

Groups vi-ix are related primarily by their subject matter— the materials dealt with or the occupations concerned. It is true that similarity of subject matter often involves similarity in method of solution. But the areas in vii include rectangles, triangles, and circles; the containers in vi, cubes, cylinders, and so on. The term "completion" is applied to two apparently quite different operations.

It looks as if the Egyptian examples were arranged for the convenience of reference by employers of labor, granary-overseers, surveyors, and brewers rather than by any logical affinity.

In Babylonia we have to rely generally on the small groups of examples on a single tablet. A Strassburg tablet contains thirty problems, all dealing with the division of triangular fields. Three could today be solved by linear equations, seven would require quadratics. Thirty-two problems are decipherable on a tablet in the British Museum. They concern: (i) masses of earth moved and the tasks to be assigned to individual laborers in complicated engineering works, (ii) the numbers of bricks walling a cylindrical well, (iii) the division of water-clocks, (iv) the time occupied by weaving operations, (v) the evaluation of crops from fields of different areas, and (vi) the height of the arc of a circle. They involve a great variety of geometrical relations. But, given familiarity with these, all the problems could be expressed either as simple proportions or as simple calculations of areas and volumes. Was the tablet's writer conscious of the inner relationship between problems superficially so different?

On the whole we have to judge the scientific value of the work embodied in our texts by its results. They disclose considerable skill in the formulation of problems. A study of the examples would accustom the scholar to arrange the data which professional practice might present in a manner suitable for mathematical treatment.

And then the examples illustrate the capacities of their compilers. The Egyptians were grievously handicapped by their imperfect symbolism and crude technique of reckoning. Though they could handle the fractions with surprising success, these must have delayed progress. In pure mathematics their highest efforts, judging by the extant examples, would now-adays be called compound proportions or simple linear equations. One of the latter may be quoted from the Rhind Papyrus (No. 34):—

A quantity whose half and whose quarter are added to it becomes 10:—

√ 1	1 + 1/2 + 1/4
2	3 + 1/2
√ 4	7
√ 1/7	1/4
1/4 + 1/28	1/2
√ 1/2 + 1/14	1

Total this quantity is 5 + 1/2 + 1/7 + 1/14

The method here adopted is just to multiply 1 + ½ + ¼ to find 10. It is followed by a "proof," which consists in halving and quartering the solution and adding the results to it to show that they do add up to 10.

The Babylonians, aided by their sexagesimal fractions could aim higher than the Egyptians and actually solve quite neatly problems involving quadratic and even cubic equations. One of the simpler quadratics may be quoted. (Note that the depth is always given in GAR, the other measures in cubits, i.e., 1/12 GAR.)

"Length, Breadth. 1;40 the length. The 7th part of that whereby the length exceeds the breadth and 1 cubit added thereto is also the depth. ;50 the volume excavated. What are breadth and depth?

You: Multiply 1;40, the length, by 12, the fraction of the depth; you see 20. Find the reciprocal of 20. ;3 you see. Multiply ;3 by ;50. ;2, 30 you see. Multiply ;2, 30 by 7. ;17, 30 you see. Multiply 7 by ;5, 1 cubit. ;35 you see. Subtract ;35 from 1; 40, the length. 1; 5 you see. Break away 1/2 from 1;5 (;32, 30) Square ;32, 30. ;17, 36, 15 you see. Remove therefrom ;17, 30. ;0, 0, 15 you see. ;2, 30 the (square) root add to ;32, 36 and subtract (it therefrom). ;35 and ;30 you see as breadth. 7 35 5 depth. The process." (The "sum" is unfinished.)

These and other technical processes were transmitted directly or indirectly to the Greeks to form the foundation of their higher mathematics. The Babylonians, for their part, remained limited by their utilitarian aims. As their generals and merchants were content with rough estimates, they remained satisfied with incorrect formulas for the volume of a truncated pyramid and the ludicrous approximation $\pi = 3$!

The movements of the heavenly bodies had to be studied by early man for practical needs of navigation and of agriculture (pp. 86, 110). Favored by the clear skies normally ruling between the 10th and 35th degree of latitude, the regularity of celestial events and their connection with mundane ones must soon have been recognized. Success in foretelling from observations of the heavenly bodies the times for harvest or the advent of a flood, then led to the prosecution of such observations in the vain hope of predicting other events affecting men's fortunes (p. 86). After the urban revolution, astronomy was still studied both for the legitimate purpose of regulating agricultural works and the connected festivals and for the futile aims of astrological prediction. The study was now supported by the authority of organized States, it was equipped with the devices the new crafts could produce, its results were recorded in writing.

In Egypt astronomy remained necessary to guide agricultural operations. It is, indeed, true that the Egyptians, probably around 2900 B.C., had devised a calendar that attempted to reconcile the old reckoning by lunar months with the solar year. But that calendar was inaccurate (p. 111) and could not be used successfully for regulating work on the farm. Attempts to reform it seem to have been made under the earliest dynasties, but were abandoned, whether through incompetence or sacerdotal opposition is unknown. But the true year was recognized side by side with the vague official year.

An inscription, written about 2000 B.C., speaks of "offerings at the feast of the Beginning of the Year, at the feast of the New Year, of the Great Year, of the Little Year. . . ." The first year mentioned is the vague official year of the calendar. The New Year is determined astronomically by the rising of Sirius. The Great Year may be a Sothic cycle of 1461 years, the Little Year was perhaps a quadrennial cycle for the correction of the calendar on the principle of our leap years. The regulation of this embarrassing number of conflicting reckonings was left to royal officials, ultimately to priests of the Sun.

In Babylonia organized observation of the heavens was still more necessary. For the Babylonians never established a solar calendar for official purposes, but recognized always a lunar year of 354 days. Even the beginnings of the months were fixed empirically. In King Hammurabi's correspondence (about 1800 B.C.) we read the reports of officials whose duty it was to watch for the appearance of the new moon. The new

month began officially only when they had reported to the king
the moon's reappearance. Charged with such a task, the royal
astronomers were naturally trained in keen observation and, in
fact, became surprisingly expert.

The lunar calendar left to itself would, of course, cause complete chaos in the community's religious life, which was bound
up with seasonal agricultural festivals. It was in practice
corrected by the periodical intercalation of an extra month.
But no system of intercalation was officially established. It was
left to the king to order the addition of an extra month to the
official year when needed. He presumably acted on the advice
of astronomers. The latter must have known the equivalent of
the solar year, but it was determined, as in Egypt, by observation of the stars.

So in Egypt and Babylonia the movements of the heavenly
bodies were systematically observed both for practical and for
superstitious ends. To reduce such observations to material for
an exact science it was essential to standardize the divisions of
time and to devise instruments for measuring them. But such
division and measurement were equally needed for life in an
urban civilization.

For work in factories and farms equal divisions of the day
and of the night respectively would be the more useful. The
Egyptians, in fact, recognized only such divisions. They divided daylight and darkness each into twelve equal watches
(seasonal hours), which naturally varied in absolute length
with the seasons. The Babylonians, on the other hand, divided
day and night, *i.e.*, the full period of the earth's rotation, into
twelve double hours (*biru*). In each case the number twelve
was probably suggested by the twelve months of the year.

For determining the hours of daylight both peoples used
the movements of the shadows cast by fixed objects. The surviving Egyptian sundials (New Kingdom and later) use the
width of the shadow of a block. The earlier examples do not
seem to be corrected for the variation in the sun's altitude. In
Babylonia the gnomon, the shadow of an upright staff, was
utilized, but no specimens survive.

For division of the night, water-clocks were employed in
both countries. The periods of time were measured by the
quantities of water that had run out from or into standardized
and graduated vessels. In Egypt the vessels from which the
water gradually flowed were conical in form, and therefore
never gave accurate results; for only from a vessel whose walls
follow a parabolic curve would the water level sink equal distances in equal times. The instrument was further complicated

by the seasonal inequalities of the "watches" they had to measure.

At first the "clocks" were adjusted by the attachment of two or more outlets, presumably of different bores. An improvement was introduced between 1557 and 1541 B.C. A high official, Amenemhat, tells us in his epitaph that he had found in earlier writings that winter nights were to summer nights as 14 to 12. He had then made his sovereign a clock with only one outlet, which gave correct divisions of the night at all seasons of the year.

This remarkable inscription attests the existence and use of collected observations inherited from earlier generations. But it also records an invention that can only have been reached as the result of deliberate experiments, conducted with a specific end in view. It is striking that the invention should be due to an official not professionally concerned with measuring time, and that he should pride himself on it. It sounds like a piece of disinterested research carried on in leisure hours by Amenemhat.

The Babylonian water-clocks were of cylindrical form. Problems in a mathematical tablet, already mentioned, are concerned with their graduation. Adjustment for seasonal variation was not needed (p. 171). But from Assyrian times we possess a table for the conversion of *biru* (double hours) into watches month by month.

Inspired by the motives and armed with the equipment above mentioned, the Oriental astronomers were in a position to appreciate even the less conspicuous regularities in the movements of heavenly bodies and to accumulate data for the construction of a mathematical astronomy.

The Egyptians mapped the heavens, drew up lists of stars, and grouped stars into constellations. The stars round the pole received special attention, and the knowledge gained seems very early to have found practical application. From the Old Kingdom the pharaoh performed a ceremony termed "stretching the cord." The traditional formula uttered by the king on this occasion has survived.

"I have grasped the peg with the handle of the hammer. I took the measuring line with the Goddess Safekhabui. I watched the advancing motion of the stars. My eye was fixed on the ?Bear. I reckon the time checking the hour, and determine the edges of thy temple. . . . I turn my face to the course of the stars. I direct my eyes upon the constellation of the ?Bear. There stands the time pointer with the hour. I determine the edges of thy temple."

The ceremony evidently concerns the orientation of a temple. Apparently its object was the determination of the meridian by observing the culmination of some equivalent of our "pole star." The success of such determinations may perhaps be judged by the Great Pyramid, whose sides deviate from true north by only 2′ 30″ and 5′ 30″ respectively! The accurately determined meridian was, of course, a base for further accurate observations.

Before 2000 B.C. the Egyptians were experimenting with stellar clocks or calendars built on the diagonal principle. Such are known only from coffins, where they have been painted on the inside of the lid to enable the corpse to tell the time! The lid is divided into thirty-six vertical columns, each representing a decade, i.e., a week of ten days, with a division between columns 18 and 19 to represent perhaps the summer solstice. Horizontally there are twelve cases, representing the twelve night hours with the line between cases 6 and 7 for midnight. The decans (constellations fulfilling the function of Signs of the Zodiac, but situated on the celestial equator), rising in the short summer hours between darkness and dawn, are entered in the appropriate cases in columns 18 and 19. They are repeated in the remaining columns in other cases lying along diagonals.

Such tables, ignoring the five epagomenal days, the different lengths of seasonal hours, and other factors, were at best far from accurate. The coffin-decorators, not being astronomers, have caricatured the scheme. Still, the coffin-lids give a clue to the knowledge possessed by the Egyptians, and how they tried to apply it. Five centuries later the tomb of Senmut is decorated with a sort of planetarium. The astronomy it discloses is not fundamentally different from that of the coffin-lids. There are several pairs of holes to denote the pole. That looks like a provision for the precession of the equinoxes. The latitude of Thebes is taken as the altitude of the pole.

Such funerary monuments are the only extant sources for Egyptian astronomy, since no astronomical texts have yet been found. They certainly embody the results of systematic observations carried on and recorded over many centuries. But they give no hint of a mathematical astronomy capable of predicting with the aid of complicated calculations. No records of eclipses survive from Egypt. Indeed, relatively little attention seems to have been paid to the movements of the moon and the planets, perhaps owing to the early adoption of a non-lunar calendar and the supreme importance of the sun god in the State religion.

In Babylonia the stars were mapped as carefully as in Egypt, and with the zodiac as a plane of reference. But the lunar calendar and astrological preconceptions directed the astronomers' attention especially to the movements of the moon and the planets and to eclipses and occultations. The scrupulous observations of these phenomena, faithfully recorded, revealed to the Babylonians regularities that are far from obvious. For instance, soon after 2000 B.C., it had been noted that in about eight years Venus returned five times to the same place on the horizon.

A thousand years or so later the Babylonians began to apply to astronomy the mathematics described on p. 160 ff., and then performed prodigies of measurement, calculation, and prediction. This mathematical astronomy lies outside the period surveyed in this book—fortunately, since it would take several chapters to explain it. Still, it must be insisted that, as in Egypt, all this research was undertaken primarily with false astrological ends in view. But it provided accurate data without which Greek and modern astronomy would be unthinkable.

Attempts at curing diseases must have been made centuries before the urban revolution. Presumably, as among savages today, early medical theory was essentially magical, and medical practice inextricably bound up with spells and prestidigitations; the account of paleolithic burial rites on p. 50 gives color to this assumption. Even so, the aid of liniments, potions, and manipulations would be invoked, and some really effective remedies thus discovered. As soon as specialists in magic arose in a society, they would be liable to monopolize the healing art.

After the second revolution we accordingly find that doctors in Mesopotamia were also priests, and in Egypt sacerdotal and healing functions were closely allied. However, Imhotep, the first recorded name in the annals of medicine, had been architect to King Zoser, though he eventually became a god of healing. The Sumerian and Egyptian medicine men, being clerks, committed their observations to writing, as did astrologers. In the Nile Valley medical books are mentioned as early as Dynasty III. Examples of such books have come down to us from a period shortly after 2000 B.C. In Mesopotamia the extant medical texts were drawn up after 1000 B.C., but some may be copies of tablets a thousand years older.

In both countries the surviving medical texts have the form of casebooks, as explained on p. 153. No treatises on anatomy or physiology survive. Yet the Egyptians in particular must have acquired very accurate knowledge of human anatomy through the practice of mummification. Nevertheless, the hieroglyphic signs for bodily organs are derived from animal, not from human anatomy. The sign for "heart" is an ox's heart, that for uterus the organ of a cow. Hence medical literature in Egypt presumably goes back to a period before mummification was extensively practiced.

Medicine was, in fact, little affected by the knowledge gained by embalmers, who formed a distinct and specialized craft. Though the heart was recognized as the center of the vascular system, the physiological knowledge implied by the texts is rudimentary. The same remark applies to Babylonian medical literature. Even in Assyrian texts the functions of the organs are often misunderstood; the bladder is never mentioned, and nerves are not distinguished from sinews.

Diseases both in Egypt and in Mesopotamia were regarded essentially as the work of demons or vaguer magic powers. Medicine therefore consisted essentially in the expulsion of the evil spirit by incantations and ritual acts. The actions, however, often took the form of the application or administration of liniments or potions. The nastier the potion, the sooner the demon would take flight; the excreta of men and of animals were particularly often prescribed. The tradition that medicines must be disgusting is a survival of the demoniacal theory of disease, traceable in the oldest extant medical texts! The same theory naturally approved of strong purges and emetics as means of expelling the maleficent agent.

Dominated by the foregoing theory, the Egyptian and Babylonian physicians had no incentive to study the objective causes of disease or to investigate systematically the functioning of the bodily organs. The theory's maintenance was bound up with all the privileges of the priesthood, so that to challenge it would be treason as well as heresy. The attribution of medical books to a god "placed medical lore outside the range of human observation as something of supernatural origin." It is hardly surprising that, beyond the discovery of a certain number of useful drugs and the recognition of a few obvious physiological truths, little of value can be attributed to Oriental medicine.

Surgery was in a different position, approximating rather to a craft than to a branch of religion. The surgeon has to treat injuries inflicted by perfectly obvious physical agencies, and has no occasion to attribute them to supernatural powers. Surgery might accordingly be expected to be freer than medicine from the domination of magical ideas, and accordingly more objective and scientific.

Hammurabi's law-code (1800 B.C.) prescribes fees for surgeons (2 to 10 shekels, where a mechanic's wage for the year was 8 shekels) and penalties for unsuccessful operations. But no surgical texts have come down to us from Mesopotamia. Is this because surgery was a craft, and craft lore was not transmitted in writing?

From Egypt we possess a valuable treatise known as the Edwin Smith Papyrus. In its present from it dates from the first half of the IInd millennium B.C., but Breasted has advanced weighty arguments for thinking that it is based on an original going back to the Pyramid Age (2500 B.C.). It confirms our expectations, in that it is free from magic formulas, records objective observations, and relies entirely on material remedies and manipulations for cures.

Like the medical texts, it is a collection of cases, but, unlike all Egyptian medical papyri, the cases are systematically arranged. They are grouped in accordance with the part affected, beginning with the head and going down to the feet, a system followed also by Assyrian medical texts and even medieval treatises. Each case gives first a classification of the wound, then an examination, by palpation where necessary, next a prognosis or verdict, and finally rules for treatment. What is most striking is that fourteen cases are described in detail which are nevertheless pronounced incurable, "a case not to be treated." The careful recording and description of injuries which the surgeon will not attempt to cure seem to disclose a more disinterested attitude to knowledge than is usual in early literature. Breasted, indeed, goes so far as to describe the papyrus as "the earliest known recorded group of observations in natural science," and to call its author "the first natural scientist."

Such a description exaggerates the disinterested character of the observations. It was plainly important to know when a case was incurable, especially if, as in Babylonia, operations resulting in death or permanent disablement were severely punished in Egypt. Still, the observations recorded are penetrating. It is noted how the dislocation of the cervical vertebrae is accompanied by paralysis and an erection of the penis. The following passage is worth quoting in full:—

"Instructions concerning a smash in his skull under the skin of his head. If you examine a man having a smash in his skull. . . . Now as soon as you find that smash which is in his skull like those corrugations which form on molten copper and something therein fluttering and throbbing beneath your fingers like the weak place of an infant's crown before it is knit, when it has happened that there is no throbbing, under your fingers. . . . Say of it 'A case not to be treated.' "

That is a very good and accurate description of the brain. The observations here recorded could not be made in the course of mummification, but must be due to the intelligent study of a wounded soldier or workman.

So far the treatise produces a favorable impression of Egyptian surgery. But if it is based on an original going back to the Pyramid Age, as Breasted thinks, surgery in Egypt will appear in much the same plight as other learned sciences. We should have no evidence for any advances since 2500 B.C. There would have been no development of the scientific spirit displayed by our unknown author, but only a slavish copying down of old results and an appeal to "the wisdom of the ancients." Of course, the absurdities of later medical papyri cannot be used as evidence for the state of contemporary surgery, but positive evidence for progress is equally lacking.

On the whole an examination of Egyptian and Babylonian "scientific literature" does not disclose such an acceleration in progress after writing had revolutionized the methods of transmitting knowledge as might at first sight have been expected. The available documents are admittedly too scanty to serve as a basis for definite conclusions. They are at least not incompatible with the forebodings expressed on p. 150.

On the other hand, literary sources do give evidence for the pooling of knowledge, of diffusion, such as has been traced in previous chapters, affecting the learned sciences. As we have described them, mathematics, astronomy, and medicine certainly assumed quite distinct forms and developed in general along autonomous lines in Egypt and Babylonia. That does not exclude the possibility of an interchange of ideas that did not affect the fundamental structure of the sciences in each country. Egyptian mathematicians, for example, could learn from Babylonians geometrical formulas without having to modify their system of notation, their terminology, or their conception of fractions. In fact, a ?Cretan medical prescription is quoted in one Egypt medical papyrus and a recipe by an Asiatic from Byblos is included in the Ebers Papyrus.

Interchanges of physicians, astrologers, and magicians between the several courts are mentioned in the Foreign Office archives of Egypt (discovered at Tell el Amarna) about 1350 B.C., and in those of the Hittites of Boghaz Keui about a century later. Soon after 1500 B.C. learned men were traveling as freely between the capitals of Egypt, Asia Minor, Syria, and Mesopotamia, as they did a thousand years later. The Foreign Office documents themselves are the results of diffusion. Akkadian was the diplomatic language of all the Oriental monarchies, and Babylonian cuneiform the script universally adopted. The Egyptian pharaohs and the Hittite kings must have imported Babylonian scribes to write it, or to train native clerks.

And with language and script must have gone the ideas embodied in its literature. The Hittites in particular did their best to assimilate all the results of Babylonian science, and drew largely on Egypt too. And Babylonian and Egyptian concepts are reflected in the earliest Phoenician documents. If the Egyptians borrowed Cretan prescriptions, the Minoans must have been far more indebted to the Nile. Long before the Greeks emerged from their Dark Age the results of Babylonian and Egyptian science were familiar on the coasts of the Aegean.

The possible range of diffusion is not thereby exhausted. The decorative art of the Indus cities, with its compass-drawn circles, circumscribing triangles, and squares, would illustrate "geometrical propositions" by 2500 B.C. Two thousand years later Sanskrit ritual manuals bear witness to extensive applications of geometry.

In the interval it is quite possible that India was contributing to the development of Babylonian mathematics. There is, indeed, as yet no positive evidence for this or against it. But much later the numeral system with a sign for 0 which we use was borrowed by the Arabs from India. The three primary centers of urban civilization and of writing may therefore have been contributing continuously to the formation of the scientific tradition which the Greeks developed and passed on to us.

NOTE ON MAGIC, RELIGION, AND SCIENCE

On pp. 50-51 we spoke of a magic rite as inspired by the same sort of reasoning as would suggest a scientific experiment. We did not suggest that the logical process was conceived as it would be in a modern laboratory, but we accepted the account given by Tylor and Frazer of the origins of magic. That is a theory of origins only, and is not meant as a description of the motives of the practitioner of magic. As a theory of origins it is not incompatible with the conclusions based on a study of modern savages—a man performs a magic rite because he believes in magic, not to see what will happen. His society is convinced of the efficacy of magic; testing is unthinkable. The attitude of the magician is diametrically opposed to that of the experimental scientist.

Again, it has been convenient to give simplified, and thus rationalized accounts of magic processes. We must then insist that neither modern medicine-men nor paleolithic artist-wizards nor Egyptian magicians did or could formulate a logical and coherent theory of magic. That is clear enough from inconsistencies of behavior which have been mentioned. For convenience only we distinguish magic in which impersonal mystic forces are directly controlled from religion in which the forces are personified, and can therefore be influenced in the same way as men by entreaties or flattery. But really there is no sharp distinction. Most rituals are designed also magically to coerce, or at least assist, the gods. That is the sense, for instance, of the numerous ritual dramas and also of the meals and beer given to the gods. It is quite obvious that science did not, and could not, spring directly from either magic or religion. We have shown in detail that it orginated in, and was at first identical with, the practical crafts. In so far as a craft like that of healing or astronomy was annexed to religion it was sterilized of scientific value.

CHAPTER IX

THE ACCELERATION AND RETARDATION OF PROGRESS

BEFORE the urban revolution comparatively poor and illiterate communities had made an impressive series of contributions to man's progress. The two millennia immediately preceding 3000 B.C. had witnessed discoveries in applied science that directly or indirectly affected the prosperity of millions of men and demonstrably furthered the biological welfare of our species by facilitating its multiplication. We have mentioned the following applications of science: artificial irrigation using canals and ditches; the plow; the harnessing of animal motive-power; the sailboat; wheeled vehicles; orchard-husbandry; fermentation; the production and use of copper; bricks; the arch; glazing; the seal; and—in the earliest stages of the revolution—a solar calendar, writing, numeral notation, and bronze.

The two thousand years after the revolution—say from 2600 to 600 B.C.—produced few contributions of anything like comparable importance to human progress. Perhaps only four achievements deserve to be put in the same category as the fifteen just enumerated. They are: the "decimal notation" of Babylonia (about 2000 B.C.); an economical method for smelting iron on an industrial scale (1400 B.C.); a truly alphabetic script (1300 B.C.); aqueducts for supplying water to cities (700 B.C.).

The "decimal notation" enabled the Babylonians to deal effectively with fractional quantities and to establish a mathematical astronomy. But place value died with their script though sexagesimal fractions survived to inspire "decimals" in A.D. 1590. Economical iron-smelting first made metal tools so cheap that they could be universally used for clearing forests and draining marshes. In temperate latitudes the new tools opened up to agriculture vast tracts of land hitherto uninhabitable, and so made possible a great expansion in population. Yet the crucial discovery was not due to the rich and long-civilized communities of Babylonia or Egypt, but to a hitherto unknown community, dependent upon the Hittite Empire.

The alphabet brought reading and writing within the reach of all and made literature potentially popular. Yet again this revolutionary simplification of writing was not carried through in the old centers of learning, but in the relatively young commercial cities of Phoenicia. Aqueducts, bringing supplies of fresh water, must have reduced the mortality among city-dwellers, and so added to the total of humanity. The earliest example yet discovered was built by Sennacherib, King of Assyria, to supply his capital.

Two of our four discoveries, therefore, cannot be credited to the societies that had initiated and first reaped the fruits of the urban revolution. Technical improvements like the addition of a fixed rudder to ships or the glazing of pottery may be neglected here, as being merely logical developments of processes initiated before the revolution. For the same reason we may ignore some medical, astronomical, and chemical discoveries made in the Orient that, purified from the dross of magic surrounding them, were incorporated in Greek science.

We are then left with only two first-rate discoveries made by societies equipped with all the advantages of the fifteen mutations that were unified in the urban revolution. Viewed in this light the achievements of Egypt, Babylonia, and their immediate cultural dependencies appear disappointing from the standpoint of human progress. Contrasting progress before and after it, the second revolution seems to mark, not the dawn of a new era of accelerated advance, but the culmination and arrest of an earlier period of growth. Yet the Oriental societies had been equipped by the revolution with unprecedented resources and a new faculty of transmitting and accumulating knowledge.

One partial explanation for such arrested growth may be detected in internal contradictions evoked within the societies by the revolution itself. The latter was made possible, it will be recalled, not only by an absolute accumulation of real wealth, but also by its concentration in the hands of gods or kings and a small class dependent on these. Such concentration was probably essential to ensure the production of the requisite surplus resources and to make these available for effective social use.

None the less it meant in practice the economic degradation of the mass of the population. The lot of the primary producers—farmers, herdsmen, fishers—may, indeed, have been ameliorated by the public works, promoted by the State, and by the security regular Government guaranteed. Yet materially their share in the new wealth was minimal, and socially they were sinking toward the status of tenants or even serfs. The new army of specialized craftsmen and laborers could certainly have found no livelihood but for the expenditure of the surplus created by the revolution. But the fraction which came to them was again trifling. An unknown percentage of the new craftsmen were actually slaves working for a bare living wage; the rest, though legally free, must have been improverished by the competition of servile labor, and were ultimately reduced to the straits described by the Egyptian father quoted on p. 149.

The substantial balance of the new surplus was retained by the few—the kings, the priests, their relatives, and favorites. Society is divided into economic classes. A "ruling class" of kings, priests, and officials is contrasted to the "lower classes" of peasants and manual laborers. The division is typified for the archaeologist by the contrast between the overpowering magnificence of royal tombs and the simplicity of private graves in Egypt or by that between the luxurious houses of merchants and the hovels of artisans in an Indus city. As compared to these the graves in a pre-dynastic cemetery or the huts in a neolithic village reveal equality, albeit equality in squalor.

Now by the biological standard here adopted the urban revolution is amply justified in its effects, even if those effects include the class division just outlined. That does not mean that such a class division was itself likely to accelerate further progress. On the contrary, it should retard it. Progress before the revolution had consisted in improvements in productive processes made presumably by the actual producers, and made moreover in the teeth of superstitions that discouraged all innovations as dangerous.

But by the revolution the actual producers, formerly so fertile in invention, were reduced to the position of "lower classes." The ruling classes who now emerged owed their power largely to the exploitation of just those hampering superstitions. The Egyptian pharaoh may have started as a magician; in any case, he did claim to be a god and spent much of his time performing magic rites. The first beneficiaries of the revolution in Sumer were the temple priests; the king, when he emerges there, is closely associated with the god whom he impersonates in periodical ceremonies. It is hardly to be expected that ruling classes with such affiliations should be patrons of rational science; they were too deeply implicated in the encouragement of hopes which experience was repeatedly showing to be illusory, but which still deterred men from pursuing the harder road of sustained and intense thinking.

And, in fact, such rulers had few incentives to encourage invention. Many of the revolutionary steps in progress—the

harnessing of animals' motive-power, the sail, metal tools—
originally appeared as "labor-saving devices." But the new
rulers now commanded almost unlimited reserves of labor
recruited from subjects fired with superstitious faith and
captives taken in war; they had no need to bother about labor-
saving inventions.

At the same time, the new middle class of scribes and
learned men was firmly attached to the ruling class. They were
in many instances actually "clerks in holy orders," and thus
as closely identified as the rulers with the maintenance of vain
superstitions. The learned professions were "respectable," and
actually offered opportunities for advancement into the ruling
class itself. Finally, the private interests of the "wise men"
tempted them as a class to set undue store by mere book-
learning as against experiment and observation in the living
world. The new sciences for which the revolution gave scope
were thus all too often fettered by subservience to superstition and divorced from the applied sciences that produced
results.

The practical exponents of the latter were relegated to the
lower classes. Escape from their position of inferiority was
not offered by technical improvements that the ruling classes
could hardly appreciate, but at best by joining the middle
class in supporting "the established church."

Thus, from the point of view of progress, Egyptian and
Babylonian societies were involved by the urban revolution
in a hopeless contradiction. And they bequeathed this contradiction to the various successor states—Hittites, Assyrians,
Persians, Macedonians—that took them as models. The cre-
ative work of the Greeks in applied and theoretical science
begins long before the "golden age," when a nominal democ-
racy had become rather a privileged minority, living largely
on the labor of aliens and slaves and the tribute of subject
states. It was when the Greeks were just emerging from the
dark age after the fall of Minoan-Mycenaean civilization that
the scientific traditions of the Orient were transformed by a
new spirit. At this time in cities already reorganized for trade
and industry, the wealth from these pursuits balanced that of
landed aristocracies but was not yet unduly concentrated,
while a simple alphabetic script made learning accessible to a
wide public.

In addition to the internal contradiction just explained, the
ancient Oriental civilizations were involved in an external contradiction of a similar nature. As we have seen, neither the
Nile Valley nor Babylonia was self-sufficing. Even when united
in a single political and economic system, each country was

forced to rely for essential raw materials on imports from regions occupied by different societies. The necessary imports had presumably once been obtained by a free exchange of surplus products. But reasons have been given for the belief that the supplies thus obtained did not suffice to meet the demands of Egyptians and Sumerians, enriched by the urban revolution.

They accordingly attempted to expedite and regularize deliveries by force; armies followed the routes opened up by merchant caravans. Eventually attempts were made to annex the sources of supplies and to conquer the exporting countries. As the rulers of Sumerian cities had aimed at giving a political form to the geographical unity of Babylonia by subjugating neighboring cities, so they sought to extend their domains by annexing geographically distinct regions essential to the stability of their economy. They came thus to embark upon a course of imperialist conquest. The Empire founded by Sargon of Agade about 2500 B.C. is the first recorded realization of this endeavor.

It is not, of course, asserted that the conqueror was consciously inspired by deliberate economic calculations. But his conquests did, in fact, tend to the results here indicated. And Sargon's empire, although transitory, became the model for all Oriental imperialisms. Throughout the Ancient East Sargon's conquests became an ideal and the conqueror himself a hero of romance. A thousand years after the disintegration of his empire, literary panegyrics on his prowess were circulating throughout the Ancient World. Fragments of such compositions have been dug up at the Egyptian capital of Tell el Amarna and at the Hittite capital of Boghaz Keui. Sargon set a standard which his immediate successors, the kings of Ur and then of Babylon, after 1600 B.C. the Egyptians, the Hittites, the Assyrians, the Lydians, the Medes, the Persians, and the Macedonians were fain to imitate.

Now these successive but short-lived empires undoubtedly contributed to human progress. While they lasted, they guaranteed over wide areas internal peace and security favorable to the accumulation of wealth. They ensured for the great industrial centers adequate supplies of raw materials. They spread abroad the economic advantages of the urban revolution and the advances in applied science that accompanied it. The ways of communication essential to the maintenance of an empire were channels for diffusion. It was along them that learned men traveled in the fifteenth and fourteenth centuries B.C. and that Greek physicians and geographers went to Babylon and Susa a thousand years later. The imperial generals themselves studied the botany and zoology of the conquered territories, and recorded their observations on returning home. Thus knowledge was accumulated and recorded.

But the instability of these empires discloses a contradiction within them; the persistence with which the subject peoples revolted is a measure of their gratitude for the benefits just recited, and perhaps of the latter's value too. Presumably the benefits were more than outweighed by disabilities. In reality an empire of the Sargon type probably did directly destroy more wealth than it indirectly created.

The first boast of an Oriental conqueror in his inscriptions is the booty in animals, metal, jewels, and slaves that he has brought home. Such plunder did not increase the total wealth available for human enjoyment. At best it effected a redistribution of existing resources and released hoarded treasures. But mostly it meant transferring wealth from poorer societies to courts already glutted with a superfluity. Thereafter the victor's main concern was to exact a regular tribute from the vanquished peoples.

In a general way the empires thus established were mere tribute-collecting machines. Normally the imperial government interfered in the internal affairs of subject peoples only in so far as was necessary to ensure obedience and the regular payment of taxes. The monarch was concerned with the prosperity and good government of his domains only if such conditions promoted the collection of revenue. And quite certainly Oriental monarchies were created by war, maintained by continual war, and eventually destroyed by war.

Now warfare has undoubtedly served as a potent incentive to new discoveries that could be applied also to peaceful ends; we saw in the last chapter how its exigencies stimulated the ingenuity even of mathematicians. Admittedly, too, militarism was necessary both to protect the achievements of civilization against the envious attacks of slothful barbarians and to spread the blessings of civilization itself. But it did not even succeed in either direction.

Despite all their standing armies and military equipment, the Sumerian and Akkadian states were impotent to repel the assaults of less prosperous and less civilized peoples. Sargon's Empire fell before invaders from Gutium, and thereafter the land was overrun in turn by Elamites, Amorites, Hittites, Kassites, Assyrians, Medes, Persians, and Macedonians.

The punitive expeditions and elaborate frontier defenses of the Old and Middle Kingdoms could not permanently protect the Nile Valley from invasion. The New Empire was founded better to defend the frontiers by advancing them. It was overthrown by the onslaughts of Philistines, Libyans, and other barbarians who had been trained in "civilized warfare" as mercenaries in the imperial armies. And thereafter the Nile Valley itself was occupied by Libyans, Nubians, Assyrians, Persians, and Macedonians. Such was the security obtained by ever-increasing expenditure on armaments and application of the maxim "the best defense is attack"!

As a civilizing force militarism's record is equally disappointing. Resistance to imperialist aggression did, as explained on p. 140, induce barbarians to adopt some arts of civilization, notably metallurgy. But in most cases they adopted only so much of the higher culture as was needed for military equipment. And that equipment was promptly turned against the imperialist apostles of civilization. The ultimate results of the "civilizing missions" undertaken by Sargon and his imitators were successful raids by barbarians on the centers of civilization; a few of these were mentioned above. And each raid and invasion destroyed men, squandered wealth, and at least temporarily put back the clock of progress.

The apparent arrest of growth, already alluded to, may be partly due to these circumstances. The period after the urban revolution is certainly one in which organized warfare is repeatedly attested both by written records and by the prominent place henceforth assumed by armaments in the archaeological record. Before the revolution unmistakable weapons of war were, as explained on p. 108, far from conspicuous. Yet it was just then that progress was proceeding most rapidly. Had organized warfare been such an essential spur to progress, a reversal of the above relations would have been expected.

And biologically the slaughter of increasing numbers of members of the human species cannot well have promoted the multiplication of that species. Yet that has been our final test of progress.

Almost from the outset of his career, it would seem, man used his distinctively human faculties not only to make substantial tools for use upon the real world, but also to imagine supernatural forces that he could employ upon it. He was, that is, simultaneously trying to understand, and so utilize, natural processes and peopling the real world with imaginary beings, conceived in his own image, that he hoped to coerce or cajole. He was building up science and superstition side by side.

The superstitions man devised and the fictitious entities he imagined were presumably necessary to make him feel at home in his environment and to make life bearable. Nevertheless the pursuit of the vain hopes and illusory short cuts suggested by magic and religion repeatedly deterred man from the harder road to the control of Nature by understanding. Magic seemed easier than science, just as torture is less trouble than the collection of evidence.

Magic and religion constituted the scaffolding needed to support the rising structure of social organization and of science. Unhappily the scaffolding repeatedly cramped the execution of the design and impeded the progress of the permanent building. It even served to support a sham facade behind which the substantial structure was threatened with decay. The urban revolution, made possible by science, was exploited by superstition. The principal beneficiaries from the achievements of farmers and artisans were priests and kings. Magic rather than science was thereby enthroned and invested with the authority of temporal power.

It is as futile to deplore the superstitions of the past as it is to complain of the unsightly scaffolding essential to the erection of a lovely building. It is childish to ask why man did not progress straight from the squalor of a "pre-class" society to the glories of a classless paradise, nowhere fully realized as yet. Perhaps the conflicts and contradictions, above revealed, themselves constitute the dialectics of progress. In any case, they are facts of history. If we dislike them, that does not mean that progress is a delusion, but merely that we have understood neither the facts nor progress nor man. Man made the superstitions and the institutions of oppression as much as he made the sciences and the instruments of production. In both alike he was expressing himself, finding himself, making himself.

The word "race," the reader will note, has hardly been mentioned in this book. In particular, in an attempt to explain, even briefly, the rise of agriculture, the foundation of States, or the growth of sciences, it was found unnecessary to invoke peculiar psychological endowments, inherited along with bodily characteristics by the human groups active in those directions. A popular theory attributes an innate "capacity for leadership" to a hypothetical "Nordic race." It would have been easy to "explain" in this way the progress of mathematics in Babylonia as due to a "mathematical talent" inborn in Sumerians or Semites. ("The Egyptians' genius for . . ." is all too often mentioned in quite serious works.) But such a procedure would not have been scientific explanation. In practice it is only a restatement in pompous language of the fact that some Sumerians were actually good accountants. At best it might mean that some inexplicable and undemonstrable mutation in the germ plasm of hypothetical ancestors, transmitted to the Sumerians, produced a brain and nervous system that facilitated the processes of reckoning.

High-sounding terms that give confusion the semblance of logic and undemonstrable postulates have alike been avoided here. We have instead tried to show how certain societies in the process of adjusting themselves to their environments were led to create States and mathematical sciences by applying distinctively human faculties, common to all men. Under certain conditions, a State and mathematics were necessary to enable men to live, prosper, and multiply. No change in germ plasm, introduced by unknown non-human agencies, had to be assumed.

At the same time, the achievements we have sought to explain were not automatic responses to an environment, not adjustments imposed indiscriminately on all societies by forces outside them. All the adjustments we have considered in detail were made by specific societies, each with its own distinctive history. In the course of its history, the society had built up traditional rules of behavior and a stock of craft lore or practical sciences. It was the application of these rules and sciences to the particular environment that determined the form of the adjustment under examination.

The differences between Egyptian and Sumerian political organizations and mathematical techniques are explicable by the divergent histories of the two societies, not simply by the contrast between the Nile Valley and the Tigris-Euphrates plain, still less by hereditary disparities in nervous mechanisms.

Now it is the social traditions, shaped by the community's history, that determine the general behavior of the society's members. The differences in behavior exhibited by members of two societies, viewed collectively, are due to the divergent histories of the two societies. But it is just this average behavior that a science of racial psychology might study; only by a perversion from its scientific aims could it deduce therefrom "innate faculties."

Actually, we have seen (p. 117 ff.) that this behavior is not innate. It is not even immutably fixed by the environment. It is conditioned by social tradition. But just because tradition is created by societies of men and transmitted in distinctively human and rational ways, it is not fixed and immutable: it is constantly changing as society deals with ever new circumstances. Tradition makes the man, by circumscribing his behavior within certain bounds; but it is equally true that man makes the traditions. And so, we can repeat with deeper insight, "Man makes himself."

Note on Chronology

DATES in years before 3000 B.C. are just guesses, and are rarely given. For the next thousand years several systems of chronology are in vogue both for Egypt and Mesopotamia. I have adopted in each country what is usually called a short chronology: in Egypt I accept the reductions in the Berlin system proposed by Scharff, and in Mesopotamia I have followed Sidney Smith and Frankfort. The dates here given accordingly differ by from 200 to 450 years from those given by Breasted, Hall, or Peet for Egypt, and Contenau or Woolley for Mesopotamia. It makes not the slightest difference to any argument in this book whether a long or a short chronology be adopted, provided it be applied both to Egypt and Mesopotamia. That the relative dates are correct for both countries I feel fairly confident.

It has been convenient in each case to follow the native annalists of both countries in dividing up history on a political basis into dynasties. In Egypt the modern practice of designating the periods of greatness as Old, Middle, and New Kingdoms has also been followed. The following table will explain the usage of these terms and dates. All dates are given in round figures.

CHRONOLOGICAL TABLE FOR EGYPT AND MESOPOTAMIA

EGYPT			MESOPOTAMIA	
Prehistoric	Tasian Badarian Amratian Gerzean Semainian		al Ubaid Uruk Jemdet Nasr	Prehistoric
2950 to 2750	Dynasties I-II			
2750 to 2400	Dynasty III Dynasty IV (Pyramids) Dynasties V-VI	OLD KINGDOM	Early Dynastic	2850 to 2350
2300 to 2000	Dynasties VII-XI		Dynasty of Agade (Sargon)	2350 to 2250
			Dynasties of Ur, Isin, etc.	2250 to 1900
2000 to 1750	Dynasty XII	MIDDLE KINGDOM	Dynasty I of Babylon (Hammurabi)	1900 to 1600
1750 to 1600	Dynasties XIII-XVII (incl. Hyksos)			
1600 to 1100	Dynasties XVIII-XX	NEW KINGDOM	Kassite Dynasty	1600 to 1150

GEOGRAPHICAL NOTE

Egypt is the Nile valley from the first cataract to the Mediterranean. The part south of Cairo is roughly Upper Egypt, that lying to the north, Lower Egypt.

Mesopotamia is taken as equivalent to the modern Iraq; it includes:

Assyria—roughly the triangle between the Tigris and the Zab round Mosul—and

Babylonia—the region between the Tigris and Euphrates south of Samarra. It is subdivided into:

Akkad, north of Diwaniyeh, and

Sumer, south thereof.

INDEX